SOARING WITH THE DODO
Essays on Lewis Carroll's Life and Art

Edited by
Edward Guiliano and James R. Kincaid

Carroll Studies No. 6

Published by The Lewis Carroll Society of North America and
distributed by the University Press of Virginia

Library of Congress Catalog Card Number: 82—83516

ISBN 0-930326-07-5

Manufactured in the United States of America

These essays appeared as a special issue of *English Language Notes,* Vol. XX, No. 2, December 1982.

Carroll Studies is a series of books published by The Lewis Carroll Society of North America. The Society publishes and assists in the publication of material dealing with aspects of the life, work, time and influence of Lewis Carroll.

SOARING WITH THE DODO

TABLE OF CONTENTS

SOARING WITH THE DODO
Essays on Lewis Carroll's Life and Art

Edited by Edward Guiliano and James R. Kincaid

Preface

The man who gave us the un-birthday had a frabjous birthday in 1982. On the occasion of the 150th anniversary of his birth, Charles Lutwidge Dodgson was honored and exhibited in ways that even the imagination of a Lewis Carroll could not conceive a century or even a few decades ago. The list of sesquicentennial tributes is extensive, and to emend an observation by the Dodo, "*Everybody* has won, and *all* have had prizes." There was a "Lewis Carroll and his Alice" exhibition at the Pierpont Morgan Library, followed by numerous smaller exhibitions around the world; *Lewis Carroll: A Celebration* and *The Pennyroyal Alice* followed by *The Pennyroyal Through the Looking-Glass* as well as many other publications; a wonderland of lectures, meetings, and plays (on and off, and off off, very far off Broadway); and much attendant media coverage. There was also that most empyreal of British nods, the placing of a memorial to Lewis Carroll in Poets' Corner, Westminister Abbey. And there is this volume.

Lewis Carroll/Charles Lutwidge Dodgson—mathematician, logician, inventor, photographer, letter writer, poet, and wit—cannot be encompassed in a single volume. There is no surrounding such a man and such achievements. The course we have followed in this collection is a series of forays against various aspects of his life and works, a series of Dodo soarings and dippings. That the Dodo could not fly need not bother us. Dodgson did, after all, picture himself transformed in Wonderland into a Dodo, and a Wonderland Dodo has great gifts unknown to the banal real thing—even when the banal thing was real. In order to enter worlds where one may "rejoice in insects" and where it is not only possible but necessary to "believe impossible things," we need all the various scholarly, critical, and imaginative equipment we can muster—and more.

FROM VICTORIAN TEXTBOOK TO READY-MADE: LEWIS CARROLL AND THE BLACK ART

Jan B. Gordon and Edward Guiliano

Photography was, in so many ways, the perfect metaphoric pastime for the Victorians; little wonder that for Charles Lutwidge Dodgson it should have played such an important role in a career filled with hobbies and diversions. It is difficult, of course, in this age of the electron microscope and the reverse angle camera to discover the meaning photography held for the Victorians. Obviously, for the man who developed the negative Hare and the Hatter of *Alice's Adventures in Wonderland* into the positive Haigha and Hatta of *Through the Looking-Glass,* who settled upon the perpetual reversability of Fortunatus' purse as the predominant dialectic of charity in the *Sylvie and Bruno* books, the principle of negative-positive correspondence, of likeness within difference, had a special place. It was Dodgson, after all, who developed a reverse handwriting that could be deciphered only with the aid of a mirror; ultimately, photography was the proof of a real looking-glass world.

Photography became a popular pastime in England in the 1850s. Dodgson's interest in it dates to 1855, and in 1856 he first purchased a "photographic apparatus." Before focusing on Dodgson's photography, we need first to look at the phenomenon of early photography in Victorian England because one of our aims is to illustrate historically what Dodgson did to nineteenth-century photography, which was to open up its possibilities. Dodgson was always pushing the medium ahead, and although he created several photographic masterpieces his achievement can never be measured by a single photograph.

One of the most striking features of photography in the Victorian period and beyond is that it is a science that had no primitive stage; it sprung almost full-blown. Whether 1828 or 1837 or 1839 is established as the birth of photography as we know it, by the 1840s there is as much detail and fullness of tone registered in a daguerreotype as there is in a modern photograph. The remarkable fullness of power born into the hands of the photographer is to be seen in the numerous exclamations of delight with which early Victorian photographers filled their diaries. Every line and crack of a neighbor's chimney was suddenly visible.[1] It was the scope of photography rather than its technology that expanded: from the undemanding still-life to portraiture,

[1]Beaumont Newell, *The History of Photography* (New York: Museum of Modern Art, 1964), pp. 22-29.

landscapes (domestic then also foreign), and finally to the documentary recording of foreign events, commencing in full with the Crimean debacle. The introduction at mid-century of negative-positive processes, which could reproduce from a single glass-plate negative a flow of prints for the market, made a significant commercial impact. The practice of exchanging *cartes-de-visite* and the vast proliferation of photographic studios (by the end of the 1850s virtually every leading town and many villages had its own photographer) are two ramifications. But, in the largest sense, they are social ramifications, affecting the distribution and availability of the new science rather than its generic development. In other words, the increasing popularity of photography parallels the increasing popularity of the novel rather than the development of the railroad or, to use a more modern example, television transmission and reception.

From the first of a series of world expositions, the Great Exhibition of 1851 in London, photography was encouraged by the establishment of display *salons* which had the effect of advancing universalism: the principle of the whole world under one roof, an idea which had its political corollary in the idea of Empire. As a harbinger of progress, of getting to know the children of Empire, it was taken up by the same scientifically-minded gentry who had provided a base of support for the study of the natural sciences earlier with specimen collecting, of which it was the visual counterpart: "The new science is par excellence, the scientific amusement of the higher classes," we are told in *The Photographic Journal* (21 January 1854).

Photography was a curiously paradoxical discipline insofar as a broadening application and interest was juxtaposed with severe albeit known technical limitations. Absoluteness of command could be achieved only within limits, so that the photographer became an emblem both of power and of power's limitations, a feature of the development of the discipline which made it remarkably adaptable to the arbitrariness that is a part of Alice's world as well, apparently, as that of her creator, if we are to believe "Hiawatha Photographing":

> Stretched his hand, enforcing silence—
> Said, "Be motionless, I beg you!"
> Mystic, awful was the process.
> All the family in order
> Sat before him for their pictures:[2]

It must not be forgotten that, unlike television technology, almost all the possibilities of the camera realized today were either glimpsed

[2]*Rhyme? and Reason?* (London: Macmillan, 1883), p. 67. "Hiawatha's Photographing" first appeared in *The Train* in 1857; the third and final version appeared in 1883.

or in a logical train of development. For example, the fixing of a moving image by a still camera—a capacity which separates twentieth-century photography from that of the Victorians—depends upon a reduction of exposure time, and progress began very early on solving that problem. From hours of exposure at first, the time was reduced to thirty or in full sunshine fifteen minutes, then to less than a minute by the 1840s. It was down to five seconds even two seconds at the time of the introduction, in 1851, of the glass negative plate coated with silver salts in collodion. This so-called wet-plate process—the process Dodgson followed exclusively—was the single greatest factor responsible for the spread of photography in the nineteenth century.

Within a single lifetime, technological development of the medium of photography was remarkably compressed.[3] While geology and biology were suggesting an ontology of development which was either part of a cosmic process (and hence anterior) or whose discontinuities were the result of the unforeseen survival of mysterious mutants, the development of photography as a discipline formed part of an alternative paradigm. And that was of a science in a sense containing its own technological potential, a model which had the added advantage of being relatively unthreatening to traditional beliefs. In the nomenclature of structuralism, the early history of photography exhibits few of the discontinuities which characterize the archaeology of nineteenth-century knowledge, but rather appears as a more or less progressive revelation of a "world" which parallels the progressive development of the potential of the media through which that very world became visible. It was a science lacking the necessary metaphor of a "beginning," and all of its attendant crises. Any photographer recapitulated the ontogenetic history of the discipline in his own phylogenetic development.

But, in addition to its metaphysical uniqueness among developing sciences, the practitioner himself quickly became an object of attention as well. Encumbered by heavy equipment, constantly gesturing to achieve an enforced silence even while bent over double, covered with Satanic black hood, messing about with strange chemicals—the process was so messy and left such stains on hands and clothes that photography was known as the black art—laboring away in dark rooms only to suddenly emerge with print, the Victorian photographer compressed in his being all those metaphoric quests for the light of

[3]See the burden of the argument by Alan Thomas in *Time in a Frame: Photography and the Nineteenth-Century Mind* (New York: Schocken, 1977), pp. 88-94. Although Thomas never explicitly discusses it, the photographer's art did not demand a large investment either in knowledge or money. That is to say, that what social scientists term "technology transfer" took place with extreme rapidity, although clearly the artistic skill lagged behind. Such was a world made for the dabbler.

truth at the end of some dark labyrinthine tunnel of investigation. (And in the process he made a comic figure of himself.) Suddenly, anyone could duplicate scientific discovery without going through the laborious research and classification of a Chambers or a Darwin. In a process which paralleled the expansion of Empire, the first "instant" science quickly came to inhabit a curious existential space, somewhere between science and sport, simultaneously appealing to the professional as well as that consummate British type, the devoted amateur, the afficionado of the hobby.

And for Charles Dodgson and Lewis Carroll, inventor of the nyctography, a bogus nocturnal memory re-enforcer, of numerous mathematical puzzles and games, of the perverse wisdom of a new arbitrary language, "Jabberwocky," of clocks that move backward, photography was the perfect discipline; as with the prepubescent child who was often his photographic subject, the camera enabled Carroll to suspend time without the discharge of endangering psychic or emotional involvement. Like so much Victorian sport, photography allowed the luxury of either active or passive participation. Lewis Carroll was the man for the discipline, and such a perfect match may well account for his genuine skill as a photographer.[4]

---

[4]An underlying theme in this essay is the appeal that photography held for C. L. Dodgson. Since we have not organized this piece around that concept, what we present is fragmented and tangential. Edward Guiliano has elsewhere summarized the general attraction of photography for Dodgson, and repeating that procedure here at some length provides a balanced view of the subject and another broad context in which to fit this essay.

Initially, the gadgetry of the camera and the photographic process may have attracted him. His interest in gadgets of all kinds is well known. His rooms at Oxford were filled with a variety of mechanical things. He owned a microscope, a telescope, eventually an early typewriter, and such unusual items as various musical boxes and "magic" pens.

Obviously his interest in photography was sustained by much more than mere mechanical intrigue. Photography provided Dodgson with an artistic outlet, an accessible channel for him to express himself visually. Throughout his life he felt a need for the visually concrete. He was always interested in the visual arts, regularly visited artists and museums, and sketched throughout his life. Somewhat frustrated by his unrefined drawings, he was able to achieve fulfillment with his photographs. He attained such high-quality photographs because his approach was that of an artist abetted by a lifelong quest for beauty and perfection. He took his photographic work seriously and often signed his prints "from the artist," and sometimes introduced himself as the artist who had done photographs the person had seen, as was the case when he first approached Mrs. Tennyson in 1857.

Dodgson's interest in the visual arts extended to the theater. Throughout his adult life he was a regular theatergoer, and in his younger days he wrote and produced some marionette plays. His love of costume photography no doubt derives from his love of the theater and from his artistic and directorial motivations as a storyteller. The impulses and techniques that result in oral and written fantasies, after all, cannot be far removed from the needs and desires of the playwright and stage director *cum* arranger of tableau *cum* costume photographer. Over the years Dodgson developed a large and diverse costume wardrobe to fuel and facilitate his interest, and he was not beyond soliciting aid in adding to his collection. In 1880, for example, he wrote to Mrs. Kitchin asking if she "*would* be so very kind as to manage the transaction" of placing an order with a hosier on the Isle of Wight; "I feel *very* shy of writing for them myself. They cannot have *many* applications in the course of a year, from clerical tutors at Oxford, for

In fact, were it not for the incredible popularity of the *Alice* books, his reputation as a photographer might well be greater.[5] Although Dodgson's contribution to nineteenth-century photography is considerable, his place in its development is often misunderstood. Gossip about the little girls and Dodgson's involvement with them, most of which is sheer speculation, tends to blur his impact upon the form of the photograph.

Perhaps the most important practical application of the new photography in Victorian domestic life was the *carte-de-visite* vogue,

---

young ladies' bathing-dresses! and they might think it odd. Have pity on my natural timidity, and get them for me" (*Lewis Carroll and the Kitchins,* ed. Morton N. Cohen [New York: Lewis Carroll Society of North America and the Argosy Bookshop, 1978], p. 34).

Dodgson's attraction to photography obviously went still deeper. He pursued beauty and purity in his art as in his life. The psychiatrist Phillis Greenacre also notes that one gets the clear impression that taking and developing pictures were a real triumph for Dodgson. When photographing he largely limited himself to idealized subjects: little girls and famous people. "It would seem that the photographs were to capture and hold as incontrovertible fact the precious moments of time and space occupied by his ideal and adored subjects . . ." (*Swift and Carroll* [New York: International Univ. Press, 1955], p. 34). Photographs exist in the perpetual present. In the continual lapse of moments they are an artificial ploy for freezing time. This technical illusion appealed to something in Dodgson, a man preoccupied with time and death. In *Alice's Adventures in Wonderland* the familiar White Rabbit, always late, always checking his watch, is Carroll's comic expression of his own, and others', anxious preoccupations with the passage of time. In real time he fretted about but accepted that all things come to an end, and in the case of child-friends that they reach puberty, grow up and generally grow away; but he also had his regrets. "So sorry you are grown-up," he wrote in 1878 to Gertrude Chataway, one of his favorite child-friends and the dedicatee of *The Hunting of the Snark,* and to her mother he continued in 1880, "I wonder when I shall or whether I ever shall, meet my (no longer little) friend again! Our friendship was very intense while it lasted—but it has gone like a dream . . ." (*The Letters of Lewis Carroll,* ed. Morton N. Cohen, 2 vols. [London: Macmillan; New York: Oxford Univ. Press, 1979], I:305 (Gertrude), I:373 (Mrs. Chataway).

Friendship is perhaps the final key to understanding the attraction photography held for Dodgson. Photography was not only an artistic outlet for Dodgson but a much-valued social outlet as well. His camera and photographic achievements gave him access to distinguished people whose company he enjoyed. Friendships often grew out of photo sessions in his Oxford rooms or at other locations, and his photo sessions provided him with some of his happiest days. His photographing of children brought him the treasured company of those he most adored and with whom he felt most relaxed.

[5]Unfortunately, only a small (but increasing) percentage of Dodgson's photographs have been published, and the same photographs are repeatedly anthologized. Often these are photographs selected because they are of special child-friends or adult friends of the author of *Alice's Adventures in Wonderland* or because they are of Victorians who are now famous. All too often artistic merit is related to subordinate status as a criterion used for selection. The result has been that many of Dodgson's finest artistic achievements are largely unknown. Helmut Gernsheim, who rediscovered Dodgson as a photographer and whose book, *Lewis Carroll: Photographer* (1949; rev. ed., New York: Dover, 1969), is still the most influential work on Dodgson's photography, must be counted among those anthologists who in the process of serving Dodgson did him a disservice. See Edward Guiliano's "Lewis Carroll's Adventures in Cameraland," *AB Bookman,* 69, No. 4 (25 January 1982), esp. 536-538.

There is a need for a proper catalogue raisonné for Dodgson's photographs. Colin Ford, Director of the National Photography Museum, England, has made plans to compile one, but no timetable for the work and publication has as yet been established.

6

which like so many social applications, tended to limit the growth of the medium. These pictorial calling cards, invariably of uniform dimension (2¼ in. x 3½ in. mounted on a card 2½ in. x 4 in.), were produced by modifying the camera to allow twelve (or ten or eight) separate images to be exposed on adjoining areas of a single plate. An individual could be photographed in a dozen different poses (for the modest price of one). Hence one's portrait could be handed out to a dozen friends and exchanged for a dozen different photographs. The *cartes* were introduced in England in 1857, and cartomania was the vogue by the early 1860s, at which time portraits of celebrities were collected alongside of portraits of family and friends and were all gathered into that most ubiquitous Victorian book and aide to polite conversation, the parlor album. A middle-class citizen leading an ordinary life among his contemporaries found a pastime that brought the world's notables into a common view (something so new then and so common now). The international display salon was domesticated, and the re-enforcement of shared values was complete. There developed a commercial trade in institutionalized figures of reverence, and later, of curiosity, as evidenced by the occasional photographic appearances of P. T. Barnum's freaks. Yet, surely, this forerunner of the bubble-gum baseball card suggests a more subterranean appeal. The Carlylean hero-worshipping temper in both Europe and America suggests perhaps an unconscious hunger for the irresistible energy of the great men of history, and the collectors of photographs of the great not only solidified and enlarged the Victorian family, but enabled one to study in the flesh the mysterious *elan vitale* or *natura naturans* which in one field or another shaped the world to will and idea. Against this background, on one hand, Charles Lutwidge Dodgson, avid collector of photographs and famed lion-hunter behind a lens, is child and father of his Age. On the other hand, it is this tradition of artless *cartes-de-visite* and stiff portraits that Dodgson deflects, opening up a different range of possibilities for photography.

The *carte-de-visite* was artless, as were some of the earlier daguerreotype portraits. Technology had its hand in this. In the case of the daguerreotypes, the long exposure times caused sitters to be clamped in chairs, extremities propped and cushioned, visages locked. Results were not much better in the 1850s; while exposure times had come down, they had not come down sufficiently to capture a sitter at ease, and also by then this sort of formal portrait served Victorian tastes as well as attitudes. Convention had taken over even to the extent that in his aspirations toward the Victorian ideal the photographer would try to make the sitter's features and positioning conform with rigid beliefs, e.g., a handsome face is of an oval shape.[6] Retouchers rode the lens hoods of photographers to fortune. If anything, the *carte-de-visite* business was worse. It *was* a business; the sitter was in and out of the vignetting chair and head-rest quickly so the next sitter could take his or her place, head fixed in a vice, told to stare at a fixed spot on the wall and remain absolutely still. When the sitter was most uncomfortable, he or she was told to look pleasant and the exposure began. There was no attempt at characterization, no attempt to record what Julia Margaret Cameron called "the greatness of

[6]See Helmut and Alison Gernsheim, *The History of Photography,* 2nd ed. (New York: McGraw-Hill, 1969), p. 235.

Figure 1. Canon John Rich (Courtesy National Portrait Gallery).

the inner as well as the features of the outer man.'"[7] The process of the passport and ID photo was born.[8]

The exceptions to this state of the craft are few. A half a dozen or so Victorian photographers raised early portrait photography from a rather mechanical process to an art. These are the photographers remembered by name, and their relatively small body of work—the

[7]Gernsheim, *History of Photography*, p. 298.

[8]This reminder of how little photography has changed in the past hundred or so years also is a reminder that, aesthetically, from the early days of the first "artist-photographers" who were active in the ten years preceding the industrialization of photography, the photographic portrait developed in two contradictory directions: one direction represented progress and the other, early revealed in cartomania, regression. See Gisèle Freund, *Photography & Society* (Boston: David R. Godine, 1980), p. 36.

Figure 2. Flora Rankin, "No lessons today" (Courtesy Morris L. Parrish Collection of Victorian Novelists, Princeton University Library).

exceptions—are rightly known today from anthologies and histories of photography. Although Dodgson is known best for his photographs of children, it is in his other portraits—many taken in the late 1850s—that we can see him rising up and striking out on his own. Placing Dodgson's early portraits alongside the stiff and conventional portraits and *cartes-de-visite* of his contemporaries is particularly revealing because in his main occupation, children's photography, there are few against whom he can be judged. Perhaps the best of Dodgson's formal portraits is that of Canon John Rich (Figure 1). Rich looks natural, real, almost comfortable. There is something to him behind a record of his appearance. He appears at ease, relaxed in the soft armchair. There are no sharp or right angles; his body curves with the chair. There is the natural positioning, the simple background, the economical use of accessories that characterize many of Dodgson's photographs. But it is Rich's face that rightly distinguishes Dodgson's portrait. There is something in the eyes, an intelligence and inviting quality, and more importantly—as Colin Ford has pointed out in praising this photograph[9]—there is that rarest of elements in this period of long exposure times, the beginning of a smile on his face. The corners of his lips are raised; not stiffly or mechanically, but naturally as if he is ready to break into a full grin. It is Dodgson's genius to coax this out of his sitters (who are really in an awkward position), and it is his genius to want to do this. It is a quality he brings to many of his children's portraits, and from Rich's photograph it is a small leap to Dodgson's extraordinary portrait of Flora Rankin, "No lessons today" (Figure 2).

From his earliest engagement with photography, Dodgson saw in it elements and possibilities that few of his contemporaries gleamed. In an essay, "Photography Extraordinary," published in *The Comic Times* in November 1855,[10] Dodgson proposes (for its comic potential) one in a series of pseudo-scientific theories; notably, that photography could be used to "develope" ideas to a required degree of intensity. Photography no longer merely captures, but is a part of development. This ideational component of the black art has obvious antecedents in nineteenth-century idealism, but more important is Dodgson's attempt to justify photography as an instrument. The development of the idea was obviously of greater importance than the mere quality of the reproduction, as concept took precedence over execution.

[9]Notably in a public lecture, "Lewis Carroll—Photographer," at the Pierpont Morgan Library, New York City, 28 January and 30 January 1982.
[10]Reprinted in several places, including *The Complete Works of Lewis Carroll* (New York: Random House/Modern Library; London: Nonesuch Press, 1936), pp. 1231-1235.

A quick comparison of his treatment of Alice Liddell, the inspiration for *Alice's Adventures in Wonderland,* with that of Julia Margaret Cameron, the century's other great amateur photographer and perhaps finest portraitist, is revealing. Mrs. Cameron's Alice (Figure 3) appears appropriately mythologized as Pomona, the Roman goddess of tree fruits. She appears as one more in a long typological succession of alluring female fertility figures. By means of soft focus, Mrs. Cameron has blurred the foreground hand, in the

Figure 3. Alice Liddell as Pomona, photographed by Julia Margaret Cameron.

process making the lines of Alice's upper torso coterminal with the contour of the arbor. As a result, the flowers appear simultaneously to be part of the tree and part of her hair. Tendrils of the tree and ringlets of her hair are in perfect balance. The boundaries between human and natural physicality are virtually non-existent. Alice appears as one more bloom amid many (as indeed typologically she is), and the predominant geometric shape is that of her heart: the plunging neckline; the lips; the forehead hair line; and the leaf shapes are all in harmony, almost as if we were looking at a Braque still-life. The internal consistency of the Cameron photograph is remarkable, and the photo is really a sequence of echoing contours that almost make us forget the girl.

There is little chance of forgetting young Alice in Dodgson's early photography of her (see, for example, Figure 4, c. 1857 or the photograph he pasted as the end of *Alice's Adventures Under Ground).*[11]

[11]Knowing the identity of the sitter in a photograph can of course have a tremendous influence on our response to that photograph. The existential bond between Alice Liddell, child-friend of and inspirator of Lewis Carroll, and the signification of a photograph of her is strong. That is to say, the twentieth-century viewer who recognizes

Figure 4. Alice Pleasance Liddell (Courtesy Morris L. Parrish Collection of Victorian Novelists, Princeton University Library).

12

His photograph of the Liddell sisters (Figure 5, c. 1861)—taken about a year before they figured in *Alice*—is part of an impulse altogether different from Mrs. Cameron's. As one glimpses this and others of his

Alice in Mrs. Cameron's photograph reads a different picture than one who does not. For the viewer who knows that Alice Liddell is the model for Pomona, much of what is regularly praised in the photograph is lost and the aesthetic experience transformed—probably becoming less intense (although this does not necessarily hold for the intellectual experience). This explains, in part, why people who come to Mrs. Cameron through Lewis Carroll have less enthusiasm for her work than is regularly awarded by photo-historians and critics. Similarly, the fixing of Alice's identity in a Carroll photograph contributes meaning and response that cannot otherwise be communicated, making Dodgson's photograph of Alice powerful and unforgettable.

Consider also what Ben Maddow has to say about the sitter in the photographic/ aesthetic process of exposure and development. "It's the special naiveté of the twentieth century to think that the artist alone determines the subject; in examining a succession of photographic portraits one is struck instantly by the will and force of the sitter. Julia Cameron's photograph of Sir John Herschel is a masterpiece not simply by her, but by this great astronomer and chemist and thinker as well. His character, and the fact that science, and therefore scientists, were beginning to dominate the life of the nineteenth century as it swelled to a close—these are to be read in the thoughtful energy of his face" (*Faces* [Boston: New York Graphic Society, 1977], p. 22).

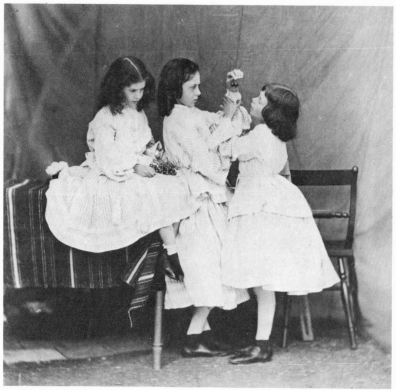

Figure 5. "Open your mouth, & shut your eyes" (Courtesy Morris L. Parrish Collection of Victorian Novelists, Princeton University Library).

photographs, several features distinguish his achievement from that of his esteemed contemporary. The young women are almost never mythologized, never participate in a typological tradition of dramatized historical women. You almost never see a Persephone or a Medusa or an Eve when you look at Dodgson's photographic subjects; instead you see the "model" invariably as exactly what in fact she is, a "model." The "pose" rather than character or will is emphasized, and it is precisely because of his positioning, the allure of posture, that his photographs have earned a reputation for sensuality in an age which invariably found ingenious means of repressing it. This process of de-mythologizing and de-historicizing his photographic subjects gives them a certain "packaged" look. Surely this is true of the remarkable photograph of Kathleen Tidy (Figure 6, c. 1861), a photograph that while highly contrived has an ease, balance and natural harmony characteristic of many of Dodgson's photographs. Dodgson's settings are never a crutch for the figures, as in the earlier

Figure 6. Kathleen H. Tidy (Courtesy Morris L. Parrish Collection of Victorian Novelists, Princeton University Library).

14

daguerreotype tradition, nor were they designed to augment some mere preoccupation or statement, but invariably exist as in fact what they are, highly self-conscious settings. There is no allegorized message "looking through" Dodgson's portraits any more than in the twentieth-century poses of models in print and film ads. Any message must be tagged by the sponsor.

The photograph of the three Liddell daughters, captioned "Open your mouth, and shut your eyes," has a highly stylized setting. The environment is clearly a makeshift photographic studio which blatantly calls attention to itself; e.g., a poorly hung back drape, a chair not needed and out of position. These are props that do not function in the photograph except to call attention to themselves as props. To be sure, the Liddell girls are the ostensible subjects of the photograph, yet at some secondary level the relationship between photograph and stage property is also the subject, just as the tree is also the subject in the Kathleen Tidy photograph. The photo calls attention to itself as an arrangement of space, as a photo and little else. One daughter (Edith) is positioned with head downward at 45^0, one (Alice) with head upward at the same angle, and the middle child (Lorina), the temptress, mediates at a 90^0 angle between her two sisters with the edible treat occupying the horizontal plane. The proliferation of table and chair legs akimbo draws our attention, by an unstated visual analogy, initially to the girls' legs, but surely also to the fact that this is an alternative meal. Not the heavy, Victorian meal with every child seated at table in his or her place (so as to ensure that all is right in the domestic world), but a meal re-organized as a child's game. The studio appears as an arbitrary setting which matches the impish arbitrariness of their meal. The photographic setting which had seemed casual and haphazard actually functions as a highly subversive setting which matches the subversive play of the children in the photograph. It is this very quality—the arbitrary nature of the objectivity of settings, laws, customs—that Dodgson's prose so often undermines for critics such as Donald Rackin.[12] Dodgson's photography at times challenges objectivity in the same way.

After a joint exhibition of photographs at Mrs. Cameron's house on the Isle of Wight, Dodgson wrote to his sister Louisa, on 3 August 1864, of his disapproval of the fellow photographer's technique: "Hers are all taken purposely out of focus—some are very picturesque—some merely hideous. However she talks of them all as if they were triumphs of art."[13] Such a response may in fact tell us a great deal about the place of photography in Dodgson's world. Boun-

[12]Donald Rackin, "Alice's Journey to the End of Night," *PMLA*, 81 (1966), 315.
[13]*Letters of Lewis Carroll*, 1:66.

daries—the very arbitrary demarcations of time and space, waking and sleep, adult and child, logic and nonsense (name and pseudonym)—were always crucial. In contradistinction to Mrs. Cameron's intended fuzziness, Carroll often artificially reinforced the lines which separate the human foregrounds from the backgrounds of his photographs (see Figure 7, for example, with its penned in outline of William Michael Rossetti's coat, 1863). Only a recognition of the necessary arbitrariness of all distinction enables the ensuing charm of their demise. In order for barriers to be broken down, their relative yet always recognizable limits must be acknowledged and maintained. Every figure inhabits its own kingdom with its own internal logic. And the artistry of each world, each language—whether it be Bruno's "oo and me" or the perverse logic of Humpty-Dumpty—depends upon a kind of isolation through which it might be tested against other versions of reality. Obviously, the photographic studio has that same monad-like quality, which, albeit isolated, nonetheless has the potential for incredible pretension. What we are suggesting is that Lewis Carroll may in fact have thought photographically, and the movement of characters through the Wonderland and Looking-Glass worlds of the *Alice* books is in fact serially picaresque in the same way that looking at a comic book is. It is not merely that the picture of the Liddell

Figure 7. The Rossetti family photographed in their garden.

sisters precedes the first telling of *Alice's Adventures in Wonderland* by a year as does the 21 June 1861 photograph of the Brodie sisters that closely prefigures *Alice*'s opening (Figure 8), but that photography and the written language were invariably thematically displaced.

Alice's Adventures in Wonderland commences as a revolution against a text; little Alice grows bored and sleepy while being read to by her elder sister, and her adventures in the magic kingdom are an alternative to a book "without pictures." At the conclusion of *Alice,* our little girl is imagined not as a rebel against the imposition of an alien text, but rather as the narrator of her own text:

> Lastly, she pictured to herself how this same little sister of hers would, in the after-time, be herself a grown woman; and how she would keep, through all her riper years, the simple and loving heart of her childhood; and how she would gather about her other little children, and make *their* eyes bright and eager with many a strange tale, perhaps even with the dream of Wonderland of long ago. . . .[14]

Alice grows, it has been suggested elsewhere, from rebellion against the tyranny of the text to a position as author(ity) behind the text, creating her own symbolic progeny, as it were, in *Through the*

[14]*Alice's Adventures in Wonderland,* ed. Donald J. Gray, Norton Critical Edition (New York: W. W. Norton, 1971), Chapter XII, p. 99.

Figure 8. Ethel and Lilian Brodie (Courtesy Morris L. Parrish Collection of Victorian Novelists, Princeton University Library).

Looking-Glass,[15] the pictorialized—in the sense that she pictures it to herself—sequel to *Alice's Adventures in Wonderland.* In that sense, her growing up is a highly self-conscious, genetic pre-version of a book such as Joyce's *A Portrait of the Artist as a Young Man.* The supplement supplants an *a priori* model in which the potential authoress had initially appeared as the victim of a text. She overcomes a previous text only by writing her own version for her own children.

Literally, but also visually, picture and text supplement one another in the *Alice* books. But also, as the creator of the New Bloomusalem

[15]See Jan B. Gordon's "The *Alice* Books and the Metaphors of Victorian Childhood" in *Aspects of Alice,* ed. Robert Phillips (1971; rpt. New York: Vintage), pp. 93-113.

Figure 9. Katie Brine (Courtesy Gernsheim Collection, Humanities Research Collection, University of Texas, Austin).

constantly reminds us, such supplements partake of a curious dialectic, a dialectic which appears to have been operative in the historical genesis of the illustrations. Because Carroll had already done thirty-seven sketches for *Alice's Adventures Under Ground* that became Tenniels' models,[16] Tenniel had to supplant his master's efforts. (Dodgson's fixed ideas and his intense, strained collaboration with Tenniel and, later, Harry Furniss is well known.) The struggle against the tyranny of historically imposed texts frames both the *Alice* books and the *Sylvie and Bruno* books. The same struggle seems to have affected all of Dodgson's children who preferred to live among pictures rather than words. Dodgson clearly liked to have a prior model when he worked, no matter what the project, be it the Queen on the pack of playing cards or his bowdlerized edition of Shakespeare.

[16]See Richard Kelly " 'If you don't know what a Gryphon is': Text and Illustration in *Alice's Adventures in Wonderland,* " in *Lewis Carroll: A Celebration,* ed. Edward Guiliano (New York: Potter, 1982), pp. 62-74. In a useful discussion of Carroll's abandonment of language for pictures), Kelly treats the impact of Carroll's thirty-seven drawings, and his text for *Alice,* on Tenniel's drawings.

Figure 10. Isabella "Ella" Maude Drury (Courtesy Gernsheim Collection, Humanities Research Collection, University of Texas, Austin).

If Dodgson as writer of texts had to come to terms with some inter-
face between picture and language, Dodgson the photographer
similarly had to come to terms with textuality. Repeatedly in his
photographs of young girls, texts occupy a metaphorical position
traditionally reserved for toys or animal pacifiers. Yet, in the deepest
sense, Carroll's photographic children are not children at all. They are
seldom dressed in Victorian children's styles (a substantive children's
clothing industry had grown up in England by the 1860s), but rather as
adults. They are almost never the victims of large, overstuffed Victorian furniture which ensured that the typical photographed child in

Figure 11. George MacDonald and Lily Scott MacDonald (Courtesy Gernsheim
Collection, Humanities Research Collection, University of Texas, Austin).

the nineteenth century remained in her place, but instead are proportionally larger than the furniture that contains them. And, for some
reason, about which we can only speculate, the angle of exposure
often gives the children the enlarged foreheads of adults (a technique
later mastered by Richard Avedon). Our attention is drawn to these
oversize heads and away from the proportionally smaller torsos (see
Figures 9 and 10 [c. 1869/70]). The large heads, the generally serious
facial expression of his children, the studious environments, and of
course the readily present "text" all conspire to create a world apart
from childhood. It is a highly literary rather than a pictorial setting.

Surely, text and picture represent two different, perhaps competing
ways of recording reality. The "text"—and we use the word in a
larger sense of "language speaking"—was essentially a mnemonic
device, a kingdom of incredible detail that was simultaneously a
repository of time. The textbook lessons in which the German dons of
Sylvie and Bruno are quite literally caught up are labyrinthically
repetitive and boring, as, apparently, were Dodgson's own lectures.
While lecturing from notes, Dodgson would occasionally doodle in
the margins the heads of those students on the verge of a flight into
dreamland; again, the very demands of the text demanded pictures.
The don, the curate, the inveterate designer of often silly word games
and puzzles, was, from another perspective, a man imprisoned by the
detail of texts. For fifty years, Dodgson kept a register of the contents
of every letter he wrote or received—over 100,000 letters. Like many
Victorians, he kept records of dishes served and the seating plans for
social luncheons and dinners. He threatened to break off relations
with a publisher of over thirty years' standing because he found im-
perfections in the eighty-four thousandth copy of a book that had
been in print for twenty years. Even with his speech impediment,
Dodgson clearly found everyday existence to be encumbered by the
obstacles that the re-production or re-presentation of thought into
language seemed to put in his way. Photography was an alternative
concept; the development of the whole picture was more or less instan-
taneous.

But, little wonder that so many of Dodgson's photographs have as
their structural center one or another book. Books and projects were
always getting in his way. And yet, just as significantly, the book,
although it may be the focus of the viewer's gaze, is never a functional
object for the subject of the photograph. In Dodgson's photograph of
Ethel and Lilian Brodie (Figure 8), a younger girl is being read to by
an elder sister. On second glance, however, we see that neither girl is
paying the least attention to the book; one is alertly looking directly
into the camera, and the other is lapsing into sleep. In the photograph

of Katie Brine (Figure 9), the oversized book draws our attention, but not that of little Katie who stares beyond it, a line of vision enhanced by a planar parallel in her swept-back hair. In the photograph of George and Lily MacDonald (Figure 11), the book at the center only seems to direct the gaze of father and daughter. In fact, his line of sight is outward into the camera, as if he were sneaking a look from the book, and Lily's is downward and to the right of the book. In essence, the book often appears (there are a remarkable number of examples) as an alternative center of attention to the camera, as in fact it may have been in Dodgson's own career. Photographically, texts function as apparent ciphers, occupying a space but never inducing attention. Even when a book is not used, as in the photograph of Flora Rankin (Figure 2), the basket of flowers is an obvious substitute, a too mature emblem of the girl's rebellion against her lessons—a companion to a grin rather than to Copenhagen's "thinker" mermaid at the left.

The predominating line of posture in Dodgson's children's photography is an arc that circumscribes some figure attitudinally between sitting and standing. Figures never seem to be entirely perpendicular or entirely horizontal, but rather positioned somewhere between. Even the girls who are seated often appear as if they were slightly

Figure 12. Elizabeth Ley "Bessie" Hussey (Courtesy Gernsheim Collection, Humanities Research Collection, University of Texas, Austin).

upright or propped with support pillows. The perpendicular lines are always displaced into soft, muted arcs (see Figure 12, 1864). As the girls are often between puberty and childhood, so their positioning is often metaphorically between standing and sitting, and it is this "lounging curve" that probably heightens the perceived eroticism. Conversely, adults often appear stunted, as in the photograph of the Rossetti family in the garden behind their home (Figure 7). The "arrested" development captures one of the predominant motifs of the Rossettis' artistic endeavors, from Pre-Raphaelitism to "Goblin Market." By stunting his subjects inside a garden littered with fallen leaves, Dodgson has produced a highly literary photograph. Again, the chronological and spatial barriers separating adult from child are so important in Dodgson's photography because of the temptation to violate those very barriers. Enlarged, out-of-perspective children (see Figure 13) look over parental space as they do in some of the constructions of Marisol. Spatial categories are re-enforced only to point up their potential vulnerability.

No consideration of Charles Lutwidge Dodgson's career as a photographer would be complete without mention of its sudden end. In 1880 when he was forty-eight, eighteen years before he died, he gave up photography for reasons that remain unclear. Although Oxford gossip about his photographing little girls "in primitive costume," as he euphemistically referred to his nude studies, may have heightened Dodgson's awareness of the potential impropriety of his hobby, evidence now suggests that it was by no means a major cause for his decision to curtail its practice. For even after 1880 he maintained an active negative file from which copies were constantly being made. In the 1890s, in fact, and up until two months before his death, he paid for Gertrude Thompson to rent one of the newer model cameras so that she could take photographs of nude models that they drew at studio sessions. And he also continued to entertain young girls in his rooms and eventually took to inviting unchaperoned child-friends to visit him for extended holidays at the Eastbourne shore. This is scarcely the conduct of a man who abandoned photography under the pressure of Victorian scandal. The answer probably lies elsewhere.[17]

[17]Current consensus points to time. Dodgson's preoccupation with the passage of time is well established (briefly mentioned in note 4). In 1880, the year his beloved Aunt Lucy died, Dodgson reached the stage in his life when he felt it was his Christian duty to complete as many writing and other projects as he could in the years he had remaining. For just that reason he resigned his Mathematical Lectureship in 1881, and within a few years he had "retired from Society," since he resented the time "lost" on social affairs. Thus in 1880, after twenty-five years of hours upon hours of devotion to his time-consuming hobby, he evidently decided to restrict his leisure pursuits, little realizing that he would, in fact, never again take up his black art.

The four nude studies that appeared for the first time in 1978 are suggestive.[18] The publication of these photos, an event eagerly anticipated by students of Carroll's work, was made possible as a consequence of the preservation of the photos by the sitter's families and are now owned by the Rosenbach Foundation. To be sure, they represent a very small sample, but are important insofar as they hint at a departure from Dodgson's other work. All four were colored professionally: one is a watercolor based on a Dodgson photograph and the other three are painted in oil. The figures are Dodgson's, but the backgrounds are not. Two are elaborate seascapes and one is set on the bank of what appears to be a river or a pond. The nude photos clearly represent a new hybrid, mixed-media form, neither entirely photograph nor entirely expressive painting. As we have seen, backgrounds

[18]*Lewis Carroll's Photographs of Nude Children.* With an introduction by Morton N. Cohen (Philadelphia: The Philip H. & A. S. W. Rosenbach Foundation). A subsequent trade edition was published as *Lewis Carroll, Photographer of Children: Four Nude Studies* (New York: Clarkson N. Potter, 1979).

Figure 13. Alice Emily Donkin (Courtesy Gernsheim Collection, Humanities Research Collection, University of Texas, Austin).

24

were always an important component, thematically, of Lewis Carroll's photographs, and it is intriguing that in his most mature achievement in the medium, he removed his children to someone else's wonderland (see Figure 14, 1880).[19]

Do these photos represent some kind of ultimate attempt at insulating his children from worldly taint and in the process finally creating painterly rather than textualized children? In which case, the last photographs could be seen as a culminating effort to depict

[19]We know frustratingly little about Dodgson's nude photographs. There is nothing uncommon about hand-colored photographs in pre-kodacolor days, or even in having a painting or drawing made from a photograph. But we have little evidence of his intentions and regard for his nude photographs, and can only speculate on whether the painted backgrounds were done to his specifications or were the conception and execution of Miss Bond, the colorist he employed (by mail).

Figure 14. Annie and Frances Henderson (Courtesy Rosenbach Foundation and by permission of the C. L. Dodgson Estate).

children who were really children, in contradistinction to so many other Victorian illustrators. Or was it, as we would like to believe, an attempt by the man who had pushed photography beyond the limitations of the *carte-de-visite,* to push it one more step ahead? For the four nude studies are in the largest sense "ready-mades"; each juxtaposes two radically different aesthetic contexts in order to force the viewer into simultaneous apprehension of an illogical relationship. The hand-done color backgrounds tend to rob the children of their naive purpose and identity in the same way in which the surrealists were later to deliberately juxtapose alien elements, so as to forever violate the immunity of the eye conditioned to regard only certain framed contexts as aesthetic.[20] And secondarily, the nude photos are evidence of a kind of automatism, both associative and recombinant, which creates a *construction* out of an *exposure.* The author who in his written work had conceptualized "soft time" long before the liquid watches of Dali, de Chirico, and Max Ernst was in the same way altering our images of innocence—the nude child—by altering its visual habitat. By emphasizing only then to obfuscate the boundaries between expression and representation, Lewis Carroll was putting a moustache on all the Victorian "Mona Lisas"—the Lily's and Alice's of another age—and in the process showing himself to be a harbinger of the next.

[20]The best elaboration of the notion that Dodgson was a precursor of surrealism, at least in his prose, is the essay by Jeffrey Stern, "Lewis Carroll and the Surrealists," in *Lewis Carroll: A Celebration,* ed. Edward Guiliano (New York: Potter, 1982), pp. 132-153.

LOVE AND DEATH IN CARROLL'S *ALICES*

Donald Rackin

I

Considering the internal and external evidence, most readers new to Lewis Carroll would naturally expect to find love playing a major role in the central narratives of his *Alices*. *Wonderland* ends (as does *Alice's Adventures Under Ground*) with remarks about Alice's "simple and loving heart"; and *Through the Looking-Glass* begins with a poem declaring that Charles Dodgson's "love-gift of a fairy-tale" will elicit a "loving smile" from his dearest little reader, his beloved companion and model Alice Liddell.[1] For Dodgson devoted a great measure of his energy in a life-long service to his love for little girls. Moreover, as a true amateur par excellence, in his everyday affairs and amusements, and throughout his letters, diaries and lesser literary works—from the satirical "Love's Railway Guide" of his juvenilia to his final maudlin opus *Sylvie and Bruno Concluded* (which ends with an angel's voice whispering "IT IS LOVE")—love was clearly one of his dominant concerns. As Dodgson wrote to an eleven-year-old correspondent when he was fifty-nine, "*love* is the best thing in all the world."[2]

Lewis Carroll is of course Dodgson's "own invention" (if you want to see him as he sometimes imagined himself, look at the frontispiece to *Looking-Glass*), as are Alice and the White Knight. But in real life, too, Dodgson played a genuine Christian knight, giving much of himself gratuitously in authentic, loving generosity to the countless Alices, Ediths and Ethels of his wide acquaintance.[3] Love itself was also a crucial topic in Dodgson's milieu, a world where, in fact, some despairing Oxford contemporaries had already turned to love as the only possible refuge on the "darkling plain" of their faithless age ("Dover Beach," incidentally, was published just about halfway between *Wonderland* and *Through the Looking-Glass*).

Furthermore, the *Alice* adventures themselves offer a variety of internal evidence perhaps more convincing than these biographical and

[1] All quotations from *Alice's Adventures in Wonderland* and *Through the Looking-Glass* are based on the texts in *Alice in Wonderland: Authoritative Texts of Alice's Adventures in Wonderland, Through the Looking-Glass, The Hunting of the Snark*, ed. Donald Gray (New York, 1971).
[2] *The Letters of Lewis Carroll*, ed. Morton N. Cohen (New York, 1979), p. 869. (Hereafter cited as *Letters*.)
[3] In her recent, provocative biography, Anne Clark stresses love as a formative element in Dodgson's character and makes a rather convincing case that Dodgson wanted to marry Alice Liddell. See Clark's *Lewis Carroll: A Biography* (New York, 1979).

historical facts or than the books' rather sentimental frames (whose relations to the actual adventures remain somewhat problematical), evidence that would also lead readers to expect more on the subject of love from these works. After all, THE KING AND QUEEN OF HEARTS stand prominently at the center of the punning world of Wonderland, and a spirit of love is expected to inform the audience's emotional response to a child protagonist like Alice. Love also lies at the base of several of those important nursery rhymes Alice unwittingly subverts. And despite the Cheshire Cat's assertion that madness reigns in Wonderland, the Ugly Duchess declares with equal finality, " 'Tis love, 'tis love, that makes the world go round!''

But Alice herself, in much the same uncontrollable way that she twists the loving and sentimental messages of her nursery rhymes into dark visions of unloving, predatory, post-Darwinian nature, reminds the insincere Duchess of the Duchess's own earlier declaration: the world goes round, Alice suggests, "by everybody minding their own business!'' Indeed, Alice's curt, unloving deflation of love here mirrors an important facet of Carroll's characteristically unsentimental wit, particularly as it works within the *Alices.* Despite the great loving care Dodgson expended in preparing the beautiful *Under Ground* manuscript as a love-gift for his dear Alice Liddell, near the manuscript's end he carefully placed his final drawing—the mad Queen of Hearts, in his own later estimate a heartless "blind and aimless Fury,''[4] as alien from love and love-gifts as any fantasy creature could conceivably be. Inside the *Alice* books, love seems to have no better prospect for survival than do any of the other admirable motives and principles that underlie and make our world go round, and that fall so easily to cool Carrollian wit and satire in the nonsensical madhouses of Dodgson's invention.

The quest structures of the *Alices* offer graphic representations of a failed search for the warm joy and security of love. Once inside Wonderland, Alice desperately seeks to enter the "loveliest garden you ever saw''[5]—that is, for almost everyone in Carroll's original audience, the Garden of Eden. But instead of a tranquil, secluded place of perfect love, the Queen of Hearts' Croquet Grounds turn out to be the grounds for perfect (albeit laughable) hate and fury—like a comic Blakean Garden of Love, an ironically perverted, dreadfully confused and threatening version of the paradise the child in us seeks in its joys and desires. In *Through the Looking-Glass*—a very different sort of

[4]Lewis Carroll, "*Alice* on the Stage,'' in *The Theatre,* 1887. Reprinted in Gray, p. 283.
[5]*The Oxford English Dictionary* (1971) lists a number of definitions of "lovely'' that, although generally obsolete today, might have been operative in Dodgson's mind in 1862: "loving, kind, affectionate''; "lovable, worthy of love, suited to attract love.''

book and one containing several positive but fleeting images of love—Alice's quest for Queenhood does not meet with exactly the same frustration, although it too ends in "dreadful confusion" which Alice must escape because she "ca'n't stand [it] any longer!" In any case, being a Queen, Alice discovers, offers neither the security of attachment nor the sovereignty of freedom to which she refers in her opening words to the White Knight: "I don't want to be anybody's prisoner. I want to be a Queen." Finally, then, Alice's worlds under the ground and inside the mirror turn out, it seems, to be nonsensical places without love, places of sheer and terrifying loneliness: in both, Alice cries bitter tears engendered by that loneliness. "I am so *very* tired of being all alone here!" she sobs in Wonderland; and with a "melancholy voice" behind the looking-glass, she cries, "it is so *very* lonely here!"

These apparent contradictions between text and context and within the text itself raise some important critical questions, among them these: Why, in view of Carroll's declared purposes for his *Alice* books and in view of other, abundant evidence (literary, historical, and biographical), do the *Alice* narratives seem to frustrate all impulses towards love—even the impulses their own frames excite? Why does love within the *Alices* exist, apparently, only fitfully and only in self-centered, infantile forms or in places where, so to speak, things have no names? More specifically, how can these beloved masterpieces of our literature be surrounded by so many frames of human love and yet apparently exclude love from their central stories? Finally, why do adult readers today often remember the *Alices,* despite all this evidence to the contrary, as somehow warm, even loving, experiences and Alice herself as the embodiment of Dodgson's own later vision of her:

> What wert thou, dream-Alice, in thy foster-father's
> eyes? How shall he picture thee? Loving, first,
> loving and gentle: loving as a dog (forgive the
> prosaic simile, but I know no earthly love so
> pure and perfect), and gentle as a fawn. . . .[6]

---

[6]Carroll, "*Alice* on the Stage," in Gray, p. 283. This highly sentimentalized view of Alice's nature is not of course always sustained by the evidence in the *Alice* texts. Several shrewd critics have in their penetrating analyses made a point of delineating Alice's flaws and shortcomings. See, for example, James R. Kincaid, "Alice's Invasion of Wonderland," *PMLA,* 88, No. 1 (January 1973), 92-99; Nina Auerbach, "Alice in Wonderland: A Curious Child," *Victorian Studies,* 17 (September 1973), 31-47; and Peter Heath, "Introduction" to *The Philosopher's Alice* (New York, 1974). Carroll himself joked, just two short years after the publication of *Wonderland,* that his book about Alice was, he thought, about "malice"—*A Selection from the Letters of Lewis Carroll to his Child-Friends,* ed. Evelyn Hatch (London, 1933), p. 48.

II

Elizabeth Sewell's celebrated study of Carroll and Lear, *The Field of Nonsense,*[7] explains why love has no place in nonsense, why, indeed, love and nonsense are ultimately incompatible. Basically, Sewell's argument rests on the firm premise that nonsense is game; consequently, *Alice in Wonderland* and *Through the Looking-Glass* (for Sewell, eminent examples of English nonsense) must turn all life, all fluid human emotions, everything, into cold, discrete, static counters for play within a closed field. The nonsense world inside the *Alices,* claims Sewell, "is not a universe of things but of words and ways of using them, plus a certain amount of pictorial illustration. . . . In Nonsense all the world is paper and all the seas are ink" (p. 17).[8]

Bearing in mind that the games in Carroll's *Alices* often involve kinetic, changing counters, rather than the static ones required for the game of nonsense postulated by Sewell (and accepted by diverse critics as an apt description of Carroll's chief comic power);[9] keeping in mind, for example, those wriggling, live-animal mallets and live-animal balls of Wonderland croquet, we can nevertheless pursue Sewell's argument profitably. For her, the *Alices* constitute, finally, "a work about itself" (pp. 21-22). Thus, love—whether as a serious subject or as a substantial conceptual element with more than mere game-counter applications, or as the spirit (style, tone, manner, etc.) in which the game of nonsense is played—has no place whatsoever in, indeed is destructive of, the game world we must enter when we enter the non-referential worlds of, say, Lear's poetry or *Jabberwocky.* For

[7]London, 1952. Hereafter, all page references to this book are to this edition and are cited directly in my text.

[8]The fact that Professor Sewell has altered her views of Carroll's nonsense and now sees much that is referential in the *Alices* does not invalidate my use here of her *Field of Nonsense.* For the definition of Nonsense as a literary genre that Sewell developed in her book still operates in the speculations of many of today's most sophisticated scholars of Nonsense and critics of Carroll. See, for example, Susan Stewart, *Nonsense: Aspects of Intertextuality in Folklore and Literature* (Baltimore and London, 1978); Gilles Deleuze, "Le Schizophrène et le mot," *Critique,* 24, Nos. 255, 256 (August/ September 1968), 731-746; and Robert Polhemus, "Carroll's *Through the Looking-Glass:* The Comedy of Regression," in *Comic Faith: The Great Tradition from Austen to Joyce* (Chicago and London, 1980), pp. 245-293.

[9]See note 8 above. Several Carroll critics, on the other hand, have pointed out that the *Alices* are not, technically, nonsense at all. In his introduction to *The Philosopher's Alice,* Peter Heath, for example, makes the point forcefully: "Carroll's fame as a nonsense-writer is by now so firmly established that it is probably too late to persuade anyone that, apart from a few isolated instances such as the *Jabberwock* poem, he is not strictly a writer of nonsense at all. . . . Carroll stands at the opposite pole from the true nonsense-writer. Although as a literary category the term had not been invented in his day, the proper genre is that of the absurd." I agree that in many ways the *Alices* do not belong in the category of Nonsense. Nevertheless, Sewell's views can be very useful in an empirical search for the meaning of the *Alices* and the sources of their power; for Nonsense does play an important, if subordinate, role in them.

what we understand by human love (unlike, incidentally, Dodgson's "pure and perfect" love of dog or of fawn) is fiercely kinetic, its kinesis and imperfection dominating the subject matter of Western literature since at least the Renaissance. Furthermore, human love never is (as every game counter must be) completely discrete, never fully completed, never isolated, and never merely about itself. Indeed, the Romantic sensibility in which so many of us agonize and glory depends heavily on the principle of incompleteness and on dreams of mergers between ordinarily discrete entities and selves (in our day represented most often by sexual unions; in Carroll's day represented most vividly in the operatic vision of love celebrated in Romantic fictions, *Wuthering Heights* being a striking example). A game uses separate entities as playthings; love, like imagination, seeks to dissolve separation and to engender syntheses greater than the sums of their parts (according to Sewell, "The Nonsense universe must be the sum of its parts and nothing more," p. 98).

Thus, accepting Sewell's definition, we must understand love as in a sense destructive of nonsense, as the warm emotional force that naturally resists taking the world the way nonsense presumably takes it, as simply a congeries of cold, discrete "units going one and one and one" (Sewell, p. 67). Love works like a solvent, dissolving isolation and breaking down separateness, making the world more fluid and less static, tending towards fusion and away from discreteness. Therefore, our quest for love in the nonsensical *Alices,* like Alice's nonsensical quest for the tranquil innocence of the lovely Garden or for the permanent freedom of adult Queenhood, seems therefore nonsensical too and appropriately destined to fail. Hence it appears that, as critics anyway, we must simply declare that the warm (and sometimes sentimental) love which permeates the frame materials of the *Alices* and which is sometimes ridiculed within their narratives has no place there, is finally extraneous, playing no important part in the books' artistic successes. In fact, it looks as though we must as critics declare the few bits of unsatiric or unsatirized love we catch here and there in the *Alices* to be sentimentally generated flaws in the generally pure nonsense which is their principal achievement.

A useful gloss on these matters appears in one of Carroll's minor early fictions, "Novelty and Romancement"[10] (published in *The Train* in 1856 when Dodgson was twenty-four and just getting used to his new pen-name). In brief, "Novelty and Romancement" is the

---

[10]In *The Complete Works of Lewis Carroll* (New York, 1937), pp. 1079-1088. Hereafter all page references to "Novelty and Romancement" are to this edition and are cited directly in my text.

first-person account of one Leopold Edgar Stubbs (among other things, a caricature of an overly Romantic narrator-hero in Poe's fiction), a young man with a feverish imagination and an all-consuming "thirst and passion . . . for poetry, for beauty, for novelty, for romancement" (p. 1080).

The target of rather crude Carrollian derision, a Romantic mercilessly lampooned by Carroll's anti-Romantic irony, Stubbs serves as an objective correlative for the spirit motivating the Romantic quest—the foolish, almost nonsensical young lover foolishly in love with love itself. And the cream of Carroll's rather facile jest depends on Stubbs' dim-witted belief that the "romancement" he so ardently seeks (compare here Alice's two quests or the hunting of the Snark) is to be found, simply, in a mechanic's shop on Great Wattles-street: he spies the sign "Simon Lubkin. Dealer in Romancement" and thinks he has found the dear object of his life-long quest. "Romancement" (here read "Love"), he fondly believes, can be bought like herring or glue from a working-class shopman.

The climax of "Novelty and Romancement" comes when Stubbs, "with a throbbing and expectant heart," discovers that he has been "deluded by a heated imagination": he has, in his youthful ardor, misread the shopkeeper's sign (this short story, by the way, offers a treasure trove for our current school of semioticians). What he had read on the sign as "Romancement" was, all along, merely "Roman cement." Until the climax, he had never seen the "hideous gap" yawning between the "N" and the "C," "making it not one word but two!" (pp. 1087-1088). Instead of the fused and fusing "romancement" Stubbs has hotly sought, he finds only "Roman cement," as cold and mundane a conception as the two discrete terms used to signify it (again compare the disappointing un-romantic conclusions and the awakenings to a dull reality that end Alice's dreams and quests). Stubbs is obviously from beginning to end a Romantic fool; but his "phantom hope" for "romancement," the childish dream he held with an "expectant heart," is no more foolish than is the dream-Alice that haunted Dodgson "phantomwise," or the imaginative dream-quests that motivated Alice herself—or the object of warm love any one of us might cherish in a young and hopeful imagination. Before Stubbs discovers the sad truth, Lubkin innocently tells him what the stuff in his shop is used for: "It would piece a most anything together." Stubbs of course misunderstands Lubkin's straightforward remark, thinking it refers to the spirit of "romancement," a spirit, he imagines, that "serves to connect the broken threads of human destiny" (p. 1084)—a view of human love consistent with much that Dodgson wrote in many of his letters, diary entries and imaginative works, a view of human love (and the imagination) to which most of us post-Romantics probably would subscribe.

In any case, the emotional-imaginative cement fusing the two, separate, lifeless, prosaic terms in Stubbs' poetic and "fertile imagination" (p. 1084) suddenly loses its cohesive powers and its own fertility; the frigid, isolated words fly apart into mere individual words again, mere dead counters in the unimaginative game of commerce and commercial communication. The experienced Stubbs puts it neatly at the end, without for once his florid and poetic prose, "the dream was over" (p. 1088). Like a reversed mirror-image of the ends of Alice's dream-quests, like the apparent relationships between the poetic, Romantic frames of the *Alices* and their satirical and nonsensical prose narratives, this ending seems to deflate love into a mere misreading of lifeless signs. As it so often does in Carroll, Romanticism here becomes a matter of poor eyesight. The coherent, unitary vision of a coherent, dynamic world alive and turning on the power of love is shattered into the dreadful but business-like perception of a "real" world of "broken threads" that goes round because each separate entity and each separate word remains separate, minding its "own business," while each seeker of love's coherence remains a fool permanently isolated in a solitary and loveless prison.[11]

Preposterous as it might seem, then, we find ourselves at this point apparently forced by firm and varied evidence to conclude that the supreme and loving creations of a man whose life and religious devotion circled around love have themselves internally little to do with love—except to treat it where it occurs with the same cold mockery they turn on all the other fond fictions and groundless imaginative constructs that help make our mad world livable. Our quest for love inside these texts seems therefore doomed to the fate suffered by similar quests within Carroll's masterpieces: whether we seek it with care and hope or with thimbles and forks, love will, Carroll's great fantasies seem to say, elude us forever. The old signs, the old words declaring love's fusing magic, like the words on Simon Lubkin's sign proclaiming his prosaic wares, fall before our clear vision into their morally meaningless, discrete parts. "Novelty and Romancement" ends both sadly and comically:

> The signboard yet creaks upon the moldering wall,
> but its sound shall make music in these ears never-
> more—ah! nevermore.   (p. 1088)

[11] The title "Novelty and Romancement" contains a complicated pun that deserves our notice: "novel" and "roman" are of course the same word in two languages; "ty" can easily transform to "tie," which is very close in meaning to "cement." By Carrollian punning, then, the two discrete terms combine into one. Such comic visions of language occur, of course, throughout Carroll's writings. Here, as elsewhere, the word-play has profound philosophical significance.

III

But our quest for the sustained and sustaining music of love within the *Alices* need not end with a frustrating Boojum. In the eighth chapter of *Through the Looking-Glass* ("It's My Own Invention"), that quest yields some authentic results. And, in spite of the apparent incoherent randomness of Carroll's nonsense materials, this chapter might even suggest for the *Alices* the possibility of a satisfying moral shape.

Besides finding in "It's My Own Invention" some of the best evidence of the loving nature that Dodgson claimed was Alice in Wonderland's chief virtue, we witness in this late, concluding episode something which, in terms of our own search for love, is much more significant—a response to that loving nature in the only genuine, fully human exchange within all of Alice's adventures: a poignantly brief, disturbingly realistic farewell between a foolish old White Knight and Alice, that Knight's beloved seven-and-a-half-year-old maiden in distress.[12]

At this late and pivotal point in her adventures underground and behind the looking-glass, Carroll's imprisoned pawn-princess is freed and is now about to awaken to autonomous Queenhood (Chapter Nine is called simply "Queen Alice"). Meanwhile, Alice's thinly disguised creator Carroll/Dodgson (after surreptitiously admitting that she too is his "own invention") prepares to lose forever his Galatea as she races off eagerly and unthinkingly to adulthood and out of the dream worlds he has lovingly invented for her, worlds where real death seems almost a stranger and where her natural aging process has been slyly slowed to a Wonderland rate closer to his heart's desire—a mere half-year's maturation for something like every nine years on the other side of the looking-glass.[13] Carroll's sadly ineffectual persona, meantime, that aged and impotent prince-charming, that familiar nonsense-inventor, the ever-falling, pitiable White

---

[12]The White Knight, a proper but silly, upper-middle-class protector of young girls, is, as many Carroll scholars agree, clearly one of Dodgson's best self-portraits. Moreover, the emotional matrix of this scene is one with which any reader of Dodgson's letters and diaries must be familiar.

[13]Although Alice Liddell (1852-1934) was ten when Dodgson first told his extempore *Alice* tale (1862), she is seven in *Wonderland* (1865) and seven and a half in *Looking-Glass* (1871). The heartfelt Carrollian arithmetic here occurs in a number of other contexts. For example, Carroll writes to one of his child friends in 1876:

I want to do some better photographs of you. . . . And mind you don't grow a bit older, for I shall want to take you in the same dress again: if anything, you'd better grow a *little* younger—go back to your last birthday but one.

Letters, p. 238

Knight, sings his last song and bumbles off towards some isolated and ridiculous death:

As the Knight sang the last words of the ballad, he gathered up the reins, and turned his horse's head along the road by which they had come. "You've only a few yards to go," he said, "down the hill and over that little brook, and then you'll be a Queen—But you'll stay and see me off first?" he added as Alice turned with an eager look in the direction to which he pointed. "I sha'n't be long. You'll wait and wave your handkerchief when I get to that turn in the road? I think it'll encourage me, you see."

In this chapter, Carroll finally brings to the surface and objectifies for his readers what they have at best only dimly sensed in their journeys with Alice through the loveless realms of heartless queens and unfeeling flat characters from the worlds of nonsense game and nursery rhyme. Until now, the only possible evidence of real love, it seemed, had been so deeply embedded among the nonsense adventures that we could have easily called *lovelessness* the keynote of the *Alices*. Until this late chapter of Carroll's last *Alice,* it appeared as if the only cogent and critically defensible way for us to justify continuing our quest for love was to claim perhaps that the narrative act itself—the narrator's gentle structuring of the inherently unstructurable, separate, discrete components of Alice's dreams into a pleasurably coherent text—comprises an act of love, a love-gift that provides Alice and the reader with a fictive shape which allows them to survive with some measure of sanity in a mad world. But this seems to me an unsatisfying, overly theoretical approach to our actual experience of the *Alices.* Now, however, in the poignant passage I have just quoted, we begin to see some reason to hope for real success in our quest.

But before continuing, let us turn for a moment to Carroll's prefatory poem, specifically to a passage that promises a particular emotional immunity. The poem ends:

> And, though the shadow of a sigh
> May tremble through the story,
> For "happy summer days" gone by,
> And vanish'd summer glory—
> It shall not touch, with breath of bale,
> The pleasance of our fairy-tale.

The narrative following this promise, however, fails to sustain such an emotional immunity. Indeed, the emotional charge underlying the haunting farewell between the White Knight and Alice is so powerful it breaks through the neat nonsense surfaces of Alice's adventures, letting readers and listeners hear distinctly and directly a different but vaguely familiar tone—that nostalgic "shadow of a sigh" which, though we hardly suspected it, has, as Carroll admits, "tremble[d] through the story'' ever since Alice first followed Dodgson's White Rabbit down the rabbit hole.

The intrusion of such a nostalgic ''sigh'' subverts Carroll's own intention to give his audience a love-gift of game-like, pure, nonsensical pleasure untouched alike by any breath of ''bale'' or by any warm, fluid emotions that can threaten the static discreteness upon which the ''pleasance'' of nonsense games rests. (In Dodgson's day, incidentally, ''pleasance'' signified, among other things, [1] a pleasant, unthreatening emotional experience, [2] for him, Alice Pleasance Liddell, his real girl-love, and [3], a secluded garden.) Admitting to the field of nonsense an emotion as alien as nostalgia risks opening its pleasant seclusion to other disturbing strangers, among them Death. Here in Chapter Eight, Death is no longer a stranger, a separate word, a mere uncharged sign and discrete counter for endless games where ''they never executes nobody'' and where Death's agent Time can itself die, or stop dead forever in a mad, unending tea-party. And the ''voice of dread'' that, as Carroll's poem reminds us, inevitably ''summon[s] to unwelcome bed'' every ''melancholy maiden''[14] here also breaks through, becoming fully manifest for the only time in all the adventures, but thereby revealing it has been a dynamic element singing at the back of Carroll's tales of Alice's nonsensical experiences of life, love, death and disorder.

Carroll himself understood the threat such a ''breath of bale'' poses for nonsense games. Consciously, he believed that the approaching, inexorable ''bedtime'' his poem alludes to must not, would not play any part in the adventures themselves (except heavily disguised in such elements as the many silly and unthreatening death and sex jokes that punctuate the *Alices*). But here in ''It's My Own Invention''—the chapter Carroll apparently considered central to the book (look at that frontispiece again)—the baleful ''frost,'' the ''raving blast'' of fall and winter which is our common lot and the basis for much of our love comes alive dramatically in the comic narrative's overt and realistic portrayals of aging, old age, and falling to earth (the text alludes to the old Knight's falling at least thirty times), as well as in its covert plays on the word ''grave'' and its many references to gravity— a no-nonsense, inescapable force pulling us all down to earth and our common grave. And the tone that conveys all this, the emotional aura suffusing this autumnal scene which reaches its climax with the spec-

---

[14]This passage has of course a distinct sexual connotation. Although sex has a very small independent role in the *Alices*—indeed, I once argued that there was *no* sex in them (see my essay ''What You Always Wanted to Know about Alice but Were Afraid to Ask,'' *Victorian Newsletter,* No. 44 [Fall 1973], 1-5)—here sex is used to underscore the frightening transience of life, conflating in a kind of portmanteau bed the first flush of full human development with its last gasp.

tacle of an aged man (not a mere nonsense creature, mind you, but a *man*) singing, as his final love-gift for a departing child, his nonsense song "The Aged Aged Man," that melancholy tone we hear distinctly in "It's My Own Invention" reveals, finally and with a direct immediacy, a fundamental thematic element that has subtly informed all of the *Alice* books, making them something much more referential, much richer and more human than the insulated nonsense we might have easily mistaken them for. Paradoxically, this grave tone emanates from Carroll's fortunate failure to keep his nonsense pure, free from that "shadow of a sigh" he himself admits. The tone emanates from a deep, abiding and inescapable sense that human love springs from time and human mortality. Hardly a fit subject for the closed fields of nonsense, but just the right subject for literary works quoted as often as Shakespeare's sonnets.

Much of the love Dodgson bore for the innumerable little Alices of his own fleeting life was of a kind adult readers know well. His letters and diaries (and his lesser literary works) are fully open about that sense of advancing age that leaves us fallen "bare ruined choirs" and makes us "love that well which [we] must leave ere long." The depth and intensity of Dodgson's preoccupation with this particular emotional and spiritual experience can be gauged by the heavy emphasis placed upon it in this structurally crucial chapter, especially in the chapter's continual iteration of two intertwined motifs—old age and falling. Like Shakespeare's May-time beloved beholding the final decline of a winter-time lover, like Humbert Humbert's pitiful adoration of his indifferent nymphet fading before him into a future he cannot share, like any of the countless figures in our literature that dramatize and celebrate this notion of love springing from fallen man's doomed race against world and time, against the imprisoning Biological Trap or the "blight man was born for," the *Alice* undertexts, amidst all the surface nonsense, have whispered from the beginning of love's intimate relations with inevitable death, but so faintly and subtly that the effect is necessarily—and, I think, appropriately—subliminal. In this late, sunset chapter of the final *Alice,* however, in this autumnal and peculiarly isolated scene of final parting between (foster) father and the child he has created, the grave undercurrent themes of age, evanescent and unrequited love and youth's impatience for autonomous life become for a very brief moment the vivid mainstream and audible melody of Carroll's narrative.

Indeed, we now know that Carroll intended to intensify these themes and make them even more explicit in this chapter: With a characteristic *Looking-Glass* doubling, he meant (although he was finally dissuaded by Tenniel) to add immediately after the White

Knight episode a parallel scene of young Alice parting from another aged man—the even older, dying Wasp in a Wig, who sings a sometimes gruesome song about his own last days:

> *So now that I am old and gray,*
> *And all my hair is nearly gone,*
> *They take my wig from me and say*
> *"How can you put such rubbish on?"*[15]

But although the Wasp episode does bear a number of similarities to the White Knight section it was meant to follow, it might not appear to be about love, the goal of our own critical quest. For while the *"very* unhappy" Wasp represents the sadness of approaching death (being November behind the looking-glass, it is already well past the "unwelcome bedtime" of most wasps) and while Alice again represents impatient youth (she turns back to the aged Wasp "rather unwillingly, for she was *very* anxious to be a Queen"), readers might nevertheless find it difficult to discover in this Wasp fragment any hint of the love-out-of-death theme I have been delineating. But the distinct change Alice's polite indulgence effects in this irascible old creature should be read in the light of its full context, representing as it does the sudden engendering of warm human emotion in the coldest, most rigid and elderly figure in Carroll's extensive collection of cranky, inflexible, waspish grown-ups. In the final words of this episode, the Wasp suddenly reaches emotionally towards Alice, displaying some true civility—a delicate social sign that for fastidious Dodgson sometimes conveyed private love:

"Good-bye, and thank-ye," said the Wasp, and Alice tripped down the hill again, quite pleased that she had gone back and given a few minutes to making the poor old creature comfortable. (p. 21)

Such genuine civility—here in response to Alice's acts of genuine noblesse oblige for a "poor creature" of the lower orders (lower biologically, socially, morally)—coming so spontaneously and from such an improbable source, represents, I think, the miraculous regenerative power loving childhood offers to the dying old: a spiritual solvent that can teach us to love and can free us from our emotional and class-conscious rigidity and isolation, as it so often freed Charles Dodgson from his.

[15]Lewis Carroll, *The Wasp in a Wig: A "Suppressed" Episode of Through the Looking-Glass and What Alice Found There,* ed. Martin Gardner (New York, 1977), p. 19. Although some scholars consider this episode an unnecessary repetition of the White Knight scene, Carroll obviously did not. He saw it through the galley-proof stage and carefully corrected the galleys themselves. A probable explanation for the suppression is that Tenniel saw himself caricatured in the Wasp and chose not to join his collaborator Carroll in his loving farewell to their mutual invention Alice. Tenniel, by the way, was some twelve years older than Dodgson.

In any case, Lewis Carroll's concentration on his peculiar child-love version of the eros-thanatos principle, his bitter-sweet and sentimental vision of a fallen old man's innocent and fruitless love for an even more innocent, unattainable child, shapes many features of "It's My Own Invention." And comprehending Carroll's strategies for transforming that vision into the nonsensical parting of a ludicrous White Knight and an eager Alice—a parting that also comically announces the approaching end of his *Alices* and the approaching end of their loving inventor—will allow us to understand better the love in the *Alices.*

For one thing, "It's My Own Invention" dramatizes a strikingly realistic encounter between two human figures as familiar in literary convention as they are in ordinary life—the aged, inept, foolish and sometimes doting lover and the indifferent, impatient, lively young object of his love. Carroll naturally employs several screens, and his treatment of this traditional material differs widely from the standard comic and tragic sentimentality with which his audience was most familiar. But many of the principal elements of the convention operate in Carroll's nonsense rendition. For example, what is often emphasized in such a couple (for tragic as well as for comic purposes) is their essential incompatibility. Here that incompatibility is deftly underscored and elaborated in some noteworthy ways. Alice, for instance, looks upon the aged Knight as a laughable old fool, but she takes pains to conceal her youthful amusement and "dares not laugh" at him; she generously allows him to mistake her "puzzled" thoughts about his ridiculous invention of a Platonic pudding for "sad" thoughts about her eagerly awaited departure. The Knight, for his part, considers his sentimental and funny song beautifully sad, while, upon hearing it, Alice finds "no tears [come] into her eyes," and even he is forced to observe gently that she did not cry as much as he thought she would. From all of this emerges a subtle, curious emotional exchange, a kind of loving mutuality we have not seen directly before in the adventures and one that, on Alice's side, represents far more than just her well-bred politeness. The fleeting love that whispers through this scene is, therefore, complex and paradoxical: it is a love between a child all potential, freedom, flux and growing up and a man all impotence, imprisonment, stasis and falling down.

While the White Knight's continual falling and his outlandish horsemanship also suggest sexual impotence (his name, it should be noted, constitutes a pun on a familiar term for a sleepless night—a "white night"—in the context of these great dream books itself a mark of stasis and impotence, as well as a reference to the kinetic, waking world of love and mortality that keeps breaking through this chapter), that falling bears a more immediate and wider reference to other sharp contrasts between him and Alice, who has now attained the evanescent ability to handle, with the grace of childhood, some rather tricky matters of gravity and balance. Indeed, some of the conversation here sounds as if Alice is now the knowing grown-up and the Knight the innocent child (a role reversal mirrored in a number of *Looking-Glass* and *Wonderland* episodes). Considering his propensity for falling, for example, Alice at one point declares, "You ought to have a wooden horse on wheels, that you ought!" and he sheepishly asks, "Does that kind go smoothly?" It is this sort of second-childhood childishness, his near-senile frailty and dependence on a fickle child, that makes him here laughable and pitiable at the same time (surely an undesirable fusion in the game of nonsense). And it is the utter hopelessness of his attachment to the departing child that, I submit, makes him a haunting figure of universal reference.

When the Knight, "a faint smile lighting up his gentle foolish face," sings his parting song for Alice, adult readers might easily overlook, in all its silly nonsense, the serious, common-sensical aspects of the song and of the entire scene. But the child Alice is not nearly so insensitive—she somehow grasps the episode's strange gravity:

Of all the strange things that Alice saw in her journey Through The Looking-Glass, this was the one that she always remembered most clearly. Years afterwards she could bring the whole scene back again, as if it had been only yesterday—the mild blue eyes and kindly smile of the Knight—the setting sun gleaming through his hair . . . and the black shadows of the forest behind—all this she took in like a picture . . . listening, in a half-dream, to the melancholy music of the song.

For the open-hearted Alice has unwittingly heard the poignant, hopeless love of The Aged Aged Man that moves secretly beneath the song's surface nonsense. And, as Carroll subtly suggests, there is a reasonable chance that Alice Liddell (in her own "half-dream," halfway between her actual, listening, reading, waking self and her fantasy self inside the dream-fiction) has heard similarly that same melancholy music here and there throughout the nonsensical adventures—Dodgson's trembling, grave "shadow of a sigh" that makes Carroll's best nonsense books timeless and universal in ways far beyond the capacity of mere unreferential nonsense.

The tune of "The Aged Aged Man," as Alice says to herself, "*isn't* his own invention" as he claims; the tune (and Alice apparently identifies its source correctly) comes from Thomas Moore's "My Heart and Lute," a poignant love lyric that no seven-and-a-half-year-old could completely understand. As Martin Gardner suggests, "It is quite possible that Carroll regarded Moore's love lyric as the song that he, the White Knight [and Charles Lutwidge Dodgson], would have

liked to sing to Alice [and to Alice Pleasance Liddell] but dared
not.''[16] In any case, Alice's politely unspoken recognition of the
underlying love lyric here bespeaks her acute child's ear, her high-bred
diplomacy, and her precocious sensitivity to the oblique voice of love
beneath the nonsense of his song and, I submit, beneath all her fan-
tastic adventures.

If we join Alice in recognizing such a faint but powerful loving
counterpoint, we add a new dimension to our understanding of the
Alices. Moore's song begins, ''I give thee all—I can no
more— / Though poor the off'ring be. / My heart and lute are all the
store / That I can bring to thee.'' The White Knight's song, in turn, is
also a poor offering, like the many poor nonsensical offerings of
another aged and silly inventor, given also in tones of modest love to
an unattainable child impatient for life and ultimately incapable of
understanding the pathetic depth of such grown-up melancholy music.
Moore's singer sings of a ''soul of love'' and a ''heart that feels /
Much more than lute could tell.'' Carroll's nonsense music likewise
cannot—must not—tell fully what Dodgson's heart feels. Alice, of
course, while capable of recognizing the poignant love song beneath
the nonsense words, is, ironically, blessedly incapable of understanding fully what that curious blend of words and music tells about
herself, about the old man singing before her and about the human
condition: ''She stood and listened very attentively, but no tears came
into her eyes.'' Fortunately, only adults can hear, if they listen very attentively, all of Carroll's gravity and melancholy love. Only adults can
hear the full sad irony, for example, of this little nonsensical exchange
between innocent Alice and her experienced White Knight:

''. . . people don't fall off quite so often, when they've had much practice.''

''I've had plenty of practice,'' the Knight said very gravely: ''plenty of practice!''

Before leaving this discussion of the melancholy tone of love upon
which Carroll's nonsense tales are based, we should remind ourselves
that the oral element, the sound of the human voice (particularly, the
spoken words of a wise and kindly, upper-middle-class Oxford don,
the product of Christ Church, Rugby, and a well-bred family) can
play a major, critically legitimate role in our assessments of the *Alices*.
The fact that Alice and her original adventures grew out of their inventor's extemporaneous, oral story-telling seems to me important.
And when we add to this the fact that references to the literal occasion
for the first telling of *Under Ground* whisper here and there through
the texts themselves (the last words of *Looking-Glass,* for example,

[16]*The Annotated Alice* (New York, 1960), p. 311.

take us suddenly back twenty years to a boat-full of real Liddells eagerly and with "willing ear" waiting "to hear" Dodgson's "simple tale"), we can probably assume that Carroll wrote all three *Alices* with the sounds of the human voice constantly and vividly in mind. That assumption becomes a critical certainty when we comprehend the extent and importance of Carroll's countless stage and musical directions—here say it "gravely" (seriously and with full knowledge of the grave); there say it with "a scream of laughter." These directions can serve of course as oral performance notes for a grown-up storyteller as much as they can serve as simple modifiers for imaginative silent readers, be they adults or children. And such matters deserve careful investigation.

But such an investigation must wait for another occasion. Suffice it to say that the sense of a stable, orderly and correct voice (without the stammer from which Dodgson often suffered when talking to most adults), speaking in calm tones, and with great sympathy for its child subject and for its child audience, informs the *Alices,* guiding our responses, fusing and shaping the discrete nonsense materials with a warm and consistently loving tone. Many readers of the *Alices* today probably hear, consciously or not, that voice of love beneath the silly adventures, like the Moore love lyric beneath the nonsense song "The Aged Aged Man." And for those who do hear, that voice somehow humanizes Carroll's games of nonsense, making the whole *Alice* experience into a love-gift as worthy of the childlike teller as it has been of his countless childlike listeners ever since.

"And here I must leave you. . . . You are sad," says the White Knight to Alice; but "in an anxious tone" he adds, "let me sing you a song to comfort you." No one else in Alice's many adventures has ever addressed her quite this way. It is as if the narrator and the narrator's gentle, loving voice have crossed over some boundary between reality and fiction, between Alice's adventures and Carroll's telling of them. It is the White Knight Carroll's last farewell and last love-gift to his beloved invention Alice. After this he must, like his inventor Dodgson (who has had plenty of sad practice saying good-bye to real girls entering queenhood), continue his well-practiced falling, alone and unaided to the end. In his later years Dodgson writes to a former girl friend now about to enter the dubious queenhood of Victorian marriage:

My child-friends are all marrying off, now, terribly quick! But, for a solitary broken-hearted old bachelor, it is certainly soothing to find that some of them, even when engaged, continue to write as "yours affectionately"! But for that, you will easily perceive that my solitude would be simply desperate![17]

[17]*Letters,* p. 862.

42

"Desperate" is perhaps too strong a word here—certainly too strong for a Victorian clergyman like Dodgson, and probably too strong to describe the White Knight's own parting words and song. But "desperate" is not so wide of the mark: both Alice and the Knight, after all, recognize that "The Aged Aged Man" is full of very "melancholy music." And, in many senses, so is the nonsensical chapter that contains it. For the impending loneliness, the approaching loss of love and life for which both Dodgson and his "anxious" White Knight have been practicing so long in their inventive imaginations, is far from a laughing matter. It is serious enough to make them both seek soothing comfort and faint hope in the merest crumbs of affection from a loving child's fickle heart.

IV

Carroll's doomed attempts to keep his beloved child-friends forever "dreaming as the summers die," his brilliant deployment of "magic words" to "hold [them] fast," his perfectly composed photographs that try to fix them forever in their passing youth—all these things represent a glorious and futile struggle of loving art against separating Time, that most abused and ridiculed figure of Carroll's many fantasies. In "It's My Own Invention," Time is finally displayed openly in its full relation to the human condition, a relation usually well masked by Carroll's sprightly nonsense. Here Carroll's many allusions to Time in the *Alices* and elsewhere seem to come into sharp emotional and moral focus, offering suddenly a brief but clear and feeling vision of Time's human significance—the despised irresistible agent of our ludicrous mortality and our wonderful love.

Nearing fifty, Dodgson writes in a letter to an adult friend, "the experience of many years [has] taught me that there are few things in the world so evanescent as a child's love."[18] And because the poignantly familiar love of an aged man for a young and innocent child intensifies that evanescence several-fold, it serves as a fine symbol (in literary fantasies as well as in everyday psychology) for the evanescence and preciousness of all love and of life itself. Thus, the terribly brief encounter between a child about to experience for the first time "queenhood" and its concomitant knowledge of death's "unwelcome bed" and a loving, protecting but foolish adult who has had "plenty of practice"—that evanescent moment permanently stopped by art's saving magic—should be understood as Carroll's special message to

[18]*Letters,* p. 441.

us, his fellow grown-ups: his own, covert interpretation, if you will, of the *Alices,* an interpretation at least as graphic as the frontispiece he chose, presumably, to depict their central theme of youth and age.

Essentially, the *Alices* stop time in their surface nonsense, presenting to the child in their readers and listeners an unthreatened and unthreatening vista of seemingly endless play, play (like the Caucus Race or Tweedle brothers' battle) curiously, charmingly static and full of discrete counters within a safe, closed field. But for their adult audience they give something more: they also whisper some sad truths about the world of flux beyond that pleasant field. The walls of Carroll's nonsense are thus constantly, if surreptitiously, breached by Time and Death and consequently, as I have argued here, by the love that springs from them both. So while Carroll's love-gift of the *Alices* helps the child Alice "keep, through all her riper years, the simple and loving heart of her childhood," another voice sings softly at the same time to other ears, to those for whom childhood's dreams might already be like a "pilgrim's wither'd wreath of flowers / Pluck'd in a far-off land."

Because it breaks open the closed field of nonsense with love, we can say that Carroll's finest comedy is much better than the cool nonsense he is often credited with. Better because it is about much more than mere nonsense is about; better because it takes account of a familiar human world charged with love and fear of death. And better because it is, finally, morally superior to the most elegantly cerebral nonsense, telling us fellow humans, in tones of love, truths about our nature in a manner that somehow makes delight of our foibles and lovely, evanescent joys of our sorrows. Like so much Victorian comedy from Carlyle and Dickens to Eliot and Meredith, Carroll's *Alices* are great and good because they rest finally upon the warm, fusing morality and sentiment the Victorian age cherished as "humor"—not upon those surface games which have brought Carroll so much critical esteem in recent years, but which his own age probably would have considered mere entertaining "wit."

Therefore, Carroll is for yet another reason one of our best writers of subversive comedy, this time because of his treatment of love.[19] Like his satire, his witty nonsense often subverts love and sentimentality; of this we are all well aware. But in addition, as we might not have noticed, his love subverts his nonsense and satire. In this Carrollian world of mixed-up signs and sensibilities, the question, as one of Carroll's most unloving characters would say, is "which is to be

[19]Carroll's subversiveness has been an important subject of some of the best *Alice* criticism from the interpretation by William Empson in 1935 (*Some Versions of Pastoral*) to that of Robert Polhemus in 1980 (see note 8 above).

master—that's all.'' Dodgson, probably, would have chosen love and romance as the masters of nonsense. The more important question of whether or not Carroll would have made the same choice can be answered in only one place, the *Alices* themselves. And these wonderful adventures seem to tell us, finally, that there is no need for any masters here; indeed, neither nonsense, nor death, nor love can master the rich, fused music of all three that makes the peculiar, abiding romancement of the *Alices* so delightfully complex.

Postscript

"unless this miracle have might"

Carroll probably had the last word, so to speak, on these matters of nonsense, referentiality, time, death and love in his *Alices*—not exactly in a word, but in a picture. The last words of *Alice's Adventures Under Ground* (and of *Alice's Adventures in Wonderland,* too) are these: ''. . . remembering her own child-life, and the happy summer days.'' But between those last two discrete but resonating terms "summer'' and "days,'' at the very end of the *Under Ground* manuscript sits Carroll's referent herself, the real dream-child Dodgson really loved, the real Alice Liddell gazing from her own "summer days''—out of the 1860's and Dodgson's lovely photograph and right into our eyes.

Although this little picture was meant for Alice's eyes alone, it still can play an important part in our understanding of love and death in Carroll's *Alices*.[20] For in this haunting photograph of Alice—set into the beautifully hand-wrought, illustrated *Alice* text and joining (as well as separating) those two, final, discrete words—Carroll embodies the motives and issues that first stirred his heart to create the nonsensical *Alices* and to animate them with a special, curious melancholy music beyond the reach of nonsense. Here before our eyes, then, is his sensitive portrait of the child who is both his heroine and his beloved audience; both a creature in his fictional texts and a real child living outside them; both a thing fashioned from mere words and the living vessel for the "loving heart of childhood.'' Before us is the actual little recipient of a very precious love-gift, the only copy of one of the world's greatest fictions. Through the loving devotion of a brilliant

[20]We should recognize the open attitude towards photography current among the educated classes in Dodgson's day. Dodgson himself had no prejudices about photographs—for him they possessed the inherent capacity to make the same contributions to a literary text that Tenniel's illustrations made to his two great *Alices*. Indeed, Dodgson shared with many of his contemporaries the view that photography held all the artistic potential that fine arts like painting held.

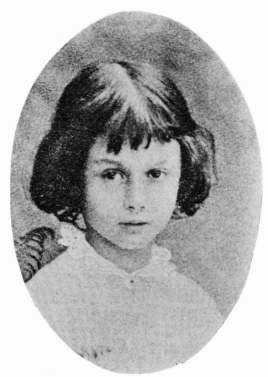

From the Collection of the Rosenbach Museum and Library,
Philadelphia.

and meticulous photographer, Alice here somehow defies Time—as if
some mad inventor from Alice's dream worlds had, with the magic of
his words and art, found a way in her waking world to defy gravity
and stop aging and death by means of an improbable Wonderland
light-machine and some Looking-Glass Roman-cement.

The *Under Ground* photograph records one discrete moment in the
actual life of one discrete child. Moreover, it records that moment
without recourse to an inevitably generalizing verbal medium (even
the precious name "Alice" is a name many can share). In the wood
where things have no names, Alice seems to find, for a moment, the
elusive love she seeks. Here in this picture of his beloved Alice, Carroll
pierces through his own verbal medium to a place beyond names and
beyond art, bringing into his text life itself and, in a real sense, the
love we all seek—embodied in one specific, very real little girl. In my
mind, then, whatever else Alice's *Under Ground* photograph tells us,
it certainly speaks the last word about nonsense, referentiality, time,
death and love in Carroll's *Alices*.[21]

[21] I am indebted to Professor Phyllis Rackin of the University of Pennsylvania for
suggesting this interpretation of the Alice photograph.

FALLING ALICE, FALLEN WOMEN,
AND VICTORIAN DREAM CHILDREN

Nina Auerbach

The prosaic but strangely haunting Alice we think we know was many Alices from her inception. Alice Liddell first coaxed her into existence, but that enchanting, unattainable child was flanked by two sisters and overborne by a formidable mother and an eminent father; our Alice is serenely unanchored even by a family name. Alice Raikes, who grew up to become an author herself, inspired the Looking-Glass world because she had the mental agility to imagine herself on the other side of the mirror, a leap of imagination which seems to have been beyond that enticing Muse, Alice Liddell.[1] The clean, blonde, primly pinafored Alice whom Tenniel introduced to the world is not the dark, sensuous brooder of Carroll's initial illustrations.[2] None of these girls is the eerie dream child of Caroll's prefatory and concluding poems, which inflate our brisk traveling companion into an abstract and awful divinity:

> Still she haunts me, phantomwise,
> Alice moving under skies
> Never seen by waking eyes.[3]

The child of the text, imperturbably civilized yet uncannily adaptable, is still another being from the inspirations and exegeses that surround her. Her aplomb makes her unrecognizable as a child, but her cool response to flamboyant violence makes her the ideal hostess for dreams and nightmares: effortlessly and instinctively, she turns madness to etiquette.

Since the original Alice was a mutable, composite creature, it is not surprising that in the twentieth century, she continues to have many selves. In the 1930s, when the horrors of Freudian analysts were infused into Lewis Carroll's gardens, Alice became in compensation impossibly pure.[4] Immunized by being a girl-child from the body's un-

---

[1]See John Pudney, *Lewis Carroll and His World* (New York: Charles Scribner's Sons, 1976), pp. 80-81.

[2]See George Sheldon Hubbell, "Triple Alice," *Sewanee Review* 48 (April 1940), 174-196.

[3]*The Annotated Alice,* ed. Martin Gardner (1960; rpt. New York: World Publishing Co., 1971), p. 345. Future references to this edition will appear in the text.

[4]Paul Schilder is dire on the "cruelty, destruction, and annihilation" of Wonderland, but his Alice is no more than its anxious victim; see Paul Schilder, "Psychoanalytic Remarks on *Alice in Wonderland* and Lewis Carroll" (1938), reprinted in *Aspects of Alice: Lewis Carroll's Dreamchild as seen through the Critics' Looking-Glasses, 1865-1971,* ed. Robert Phillips (New York: Vanguard Press, 1971), pp. 283-292. William Empson's classic celebration of the cerebral, sexless Alice is by far the richest tribute to her immunity from Wonderland's aggression; see William Empson, "*Alice in Wonderland:* The Child as Swain" (1935), reprinted in *Aspects of Alice,* pp. 344-373.

acknowledged lusts, Alice also seemed impervious of the horrors of war: the golden child about whom Mrs. Miniver read to her family during a bombing was an eternal talisman against destruction. More recently though, this impassive innocent has been seen as herself a bomb, bringing "death, predation, and egoism" into the comic harmony of Wonderland.[5] Like actual women in the 1970s, the disruptive, incipiently violent Alice refuses to function as remote redeemer. Her polite rapacity insists with the Wonderland pigeon that a little girl is "a kind of serpent" (p. 76). Rather than remaining an immunizing visitation, our contemporary Alice is herself an agent of fear.

Do Alice's many manifestations cohere into a single vision? Is it possible to unify the pure child with the predator, the blonde with the dark model, the guarded, inscrutable Muse of Alice Liddell with the avid, questing child Alice Raikes evokes? A unified vision of Alice may lie only in the complex mobility of Lewis Carroll's visual genius.

He saw and collected pictures as avidly as he invented them, hovering enthusiastically around the Pre-Raphaelites and their circle.[6] The mutable Alice who obsessed him thus took much of her contradictory life from the visual iconography of her age. As an amalgam of purity and subversive power, of propriety and holy exile, Alice is a nursery avatar of a grand Pre-Raphaelite icon: the fallen woman, scandalous and blessed.[7]

"Down, down, down. Would the fall *never* come to an end?" Alice wonders dreamily at the beginning of her pilgrimage (p. 27). For many Victorian women, as for this golden child, it seems that the fall never did. Actual, unglamorous prostitutes abounded in urban England, living vulnerable, precarious lives as scapegoats of family respectability and the Victorian bad conscience; yet majestic fallen women cut operatic figures in fiction, art, and the stage. Dante Gabriel Rossetti's *Found,* which was Carroll's favorite among his paintings, depicts a crouched prostitute as a figure of garish, irresistible grandeur, her monumentality dwarfing surrounding ordinariness.[8] (See Figure 1.) In

[5]James R. Kincaid, "Alice's Invasion of Wonderland," *PMLA* 88 (Jan. 1973), 94. Nina Auerbach, "Alice and Wonderland: A Curious Child," *Victorian Studies* 17 (Sept. 1973), 31-47, unearths a similarly aggressive Alice with more emphasis on her femaleness.

[6]Jeffrey Stern, "Lewis Carroll the Pre-Raphaelite: 'Fainting in Coils,' " in *Lewis Carroll Observed: A Collection of Unpublished Photographs, Drawings, Poetry, and New Essays,* ed. Edward Guiliano (New York: Clarkson N. Potter, Inc., 1976), pp. 161-180, is an illuminating account of Carroll's Pre-Raphaelite connections.

[7]For the fallen woman in Victorian iconography, see especially Susan P. Casteras, "Down the Garden Path: Courtship Culture and its Imagery in Victorian Painting," diss. Yale, 1977; Linda Nochlin, "Lost and *Found:* Once More the Fallen Woman," *Art Bulletin* 60 (1978), 139-153; and Nina Auerbach, "The Rise of the Fallen Woman," *Nineteenth-Century Fiction* 35 (June 1980), 29-52.

[8]For Carroll and *Found,* see Florence Becker Lennon, *The Life of Lewis Carroll,* third revised edition (New York: Dover, 1972), p. 162.

48

similar fashion, Alice dwarfs and overturns the worlds she invades. By convention, the fallen woman must writhe in tortured postures of remorse until she dies penitent at the end of her story. Alice is equally alienated, equally tortured by the writhing and disruptive activities of her own body; throughout her journeys she is the object of veiled murderous threats; in both books, she can save herself from devastation by her dream only by awakening into a vaporous normality. But like the fallen woman, Alice is a titanic outcast, dooming as well as doomed, whose fall endows her with the power to smash and transcend all rooms she enters and all countries to which she travels.

The hidden power of the seemingly inviolate Alice aligns her with

Figure 1. Dante Gabriel Rossetti's "Found."

this popular Victorian descendant of Pandora and Eve. Like that of the fallen woman in Rossetti's *Found,* who draws irresistible strength from the wall which shelters her, Alice's fall is both a punishment for her inveterate curiosity and an alliance with mysterious underground laws that empower her. Like Milton's Eve, the ever-ravenous Alice is a creature of curiosity and appetite. Eve fell through eating to become a god, and Alice, who is always hungry, becomes the creator of worlds through falling. As her curiosity causes her fall, so her hunger impels her rise: eating and drinking produce the size changes that at times place her at the mercy of Wonderland but ultimately allow her to rule it. In this loving parody of Genesis and of contemporary fallen women, Alice is simultaneously Wonderland's slave and its queen, its creator and destroyer as well as its victim. Carroll's pure little girl, so painfully careful of her etiquette, takes much of her paradoxical power from an army of women whose activities she would not have been allowed to know.

Carroll's peculiarly Victorian triumph lay in his amalgamation of the fallen woman with the unfallen child. His Alice is most insistently herself when she is placed among other, more untroublingly adorable Victorian children. It suits her to reveal herself in pictures as well as conversations, for since she is well brought up, she is generally seen rather than heard. Like the stammering artist who created her, she is more comfortable looking than she is speaking. Like many women and womanly children, she greets shock with a mask of vapidity, responding to hysterical assaults with speaking silence.

Alice's verbal decorum, her apparent translucency, may seem at first to align her with another dear Victorian child: the placid subject of John Everett Millais' famous *Bubbles.* The conceit that underlies this popular painting equates the little boy with the pastel transparency of his own bubbles, beautiful, characterless ephemera that break when touched. The characterlessness of ideal Victorian children is enshrined in Ford Madox Brown's delicate portrait of Madeline Scott, who could be watching a pastoral picnic, a rudely prying viewer, or a wolf eating her grandmother, with equal placidity. She seems worlds away from the sharp, unwomanly slash of Pre-Raphaelite fallen women, living as a series of circles, repetitively restful to the eye, suggestive of eternity or of nullity according to the viewer's perspective. While the Victorian fallen woman proclaims her existence by destroying whatever community she is part of, Brown's little girl is obediently plastic, the receptacle of any identity the viewer likes. Superficially, her demure malleability and dreamy circularity belong to the same golden vision of a purified childhood that Carroll's books immortalize.

But even as Tenniel draws her, Alice offers only a troubling repose. (See Figure 2.) Here she is at last, at her most sublimely, determinedly vacant. If Carroll had written a conduct book for girls instead of a dark, amoral dream, he might have called this illustration A Young Lady Transcending Circumstances. Like Millais' bubble-blower or

Figure 2. John Tenniel, from *Alice's Adventures in Wonderland*.

Brown's Madeline Scott, Alice is composed in a series of restful circles, forming an island of purity around the pig she is forced to cradle. But these circles enclose rather than exclude the pig, whose own bloated circularity parodies the little girl's purity. Like those of the witch and her familiar, these shapes hint at buried metamorphic possibilities whereby each might become the other; Irving Massey's fascinating *The Gaping Pig* locates the pig as the central metamorphic image in western iconography, suggesting that Alice may be embracing her own hidden potential for insidious changes.[9] Though Tenniel's Alice is sometimes jarringly mannikin-like, his composition here captures perfectly the suggestiveness of Carroll's text: a little girl is simultaneously "a kind of serpent," the epithet "Pig!" applies to all available auditors (p. 83), and a child's impassive purity is large enough to include the wriggles of indeterminate matter.

Unlike that of Millais' bubble-blower, Alice's purity does not align her with the ephemeral; like her hunger, it gives her power over size and scale. Like the grandly metamorphic fallen woman, she can make daily reality "softly and suddenly vanish away" as she unexpectedly, and threateningly, grows.

Lewis Carroll's own drawings for *Alice's Adventures Under Ground* insist upon Alice's bigness as Tenniel and his successors, whose Alice is generally more dainty than mighty, do not. (See Figure 3.) Coiled in the White Rabbit's house, as imperturbable as ever, Alice seems poised to spring as she curls into her own monumentality. Her cumbersome majesty links her less with the reassuringly vacant child of Victorian stereotype than with such awkwardly outsize Pre-

[9]Irving Massey, *The Gaping Pig: Literature and Metamorphosis* (Berkeley: University of California Press, 1976).

Figure 3. Lewis Carroll, from *Alice's Adventures Under Ground.*

Raphaelite deities as the fallen Madonna who looms towards us in Ford Madox Brown's *Take Your Son, Sir,* or Dante Gabriel Rossetti's Astarte Syriaca, an invading ancient divinity who seems about to swell out of her frame. The surprising friendship between Carroll and Rossetti may have been cemented by their shared, horrified fascination with female growth. For though Carroll often lost his child-friends once they had grown up, he was riveted by the streaks of adulthood in their youth. His photographs of Alice Liddell as a streetwise "Beggar Girl," or of tiny Alice Donkin (his brother's future wife) coolly enacting "The Elopement," expose the incipient woman secreted within the child. His culture idealized the child-woman, hymning the overgrown child who made the perfect wife, but Carroll found his main inspiration in the woman who revealed herself within the child's mask. Similarly, as his career develops, Rossetti's demi-goddesses grow increasingly enormous.[10] A chronological examination of the many versions of his *Found* discloses a wispy, starved-looking model swelling into the operatic dimensions of Fanny Cornforth.[11] In the course of her evolution, Rossetti's demi-divine fallen woman grows as Carroll's Alice does in the course of her story. The growth of each endows her with a menacing fascination.

Though as verbal and visual artist, Carroll's one true subject was the little girl, his fascination stems not from her littleness but from her potential to grow big. His photographs of his child-friends caress their subjects not in condescension to their pathos, but in respect for their latent power. The force of growth compressed within his little women is one manifestation of the Pre-Raphaelite obsession with the latent powers of impassive womanhood. For the Pre-Raphaelites, Tennyson's Lady of Shalott swells into the central emblem of power confined; Carroll locates his central explosive force in the polite little girl who possesses the vital secret of her own adult potential. It may be that this anomalous creature arose out of pained Victorian doubts as to where the boundaries of childhood lay, doubts which intensified the insulation of childhood purity in sentimental Victorian art.[12] I suspect, though, that Carroll's Alice grew out of a more poignant insight: his awareness of the fragility of female adulthood in an infantilizing life. In the ideology of Victorian womanhood, marriage signalled not

[10]David Sonstroem's *Rossetti and the Fair Lady* (Middletown, Conn.: Wesleyan University Press, 1970) is a compelling account of the iconographic history of Rossetti's woman-worship.

[11]Nochlin, 143, 147-148.

[12]Excellent discussions of the ambiguity of Victorian childhood can be found in Jan B. Gordon, "The *Alice* Books and the Metaphors of Victorian Childhood," in *Aspects of Alice*, pp. 93-113, and Deborah Gorham, "The 'Maiden Tribute of Modern Babylon' Re-examined: Child Prostitution and the Idea of Childhood in Late-Victorian England," *Victorian Studies* 21 (Spring 1978), 353-379.

maturity but death into a perpetual nursery. Thus, paradoxically, the intact child is in securest possession of the mobility and power of her potential adult future. This irony that underlay the actual lives of girls, rather than a peculiarly pathological terror of adult sexuality, animates the morbid prefatory poem to *Through the Looking-Glass.*

> Come, harken then, ere voice of dread,
>   With bitter tidings laden,
> Shall summon to unwelcome bed
>   A melancholy maiden!
> We are but older children, dear,
> Who fret to find our bedtime near.

(p. 173)

This conflation of the marriage with the deathbed, noted by Empson, suggests a double death: that of the innocent child and of her mighty adult future. The integrity of this vision of the female child lies in seeing in her not a rarefied and fragile shelter from adult experience, but a force of growth complete in herself, for whom adult life will constitute a violation of power.

Carroll's photographs of children differ from grand Pre-Raphaelite female icons in that the latter tend to be marmoreal still-lives, while the former are remarkable for their mobility, their promise of perpetual activity and change. To elicit the essence of his sitters, Carroll seems to have encouraged them to act, thus releasing the metamorphic potential he saw coiled within little girls: the hallmark of his photographs is his use of costumes, props, and the imaginative intensity of an improvised scene caught at midpoint. Carroll's love for the theater was one of the sirens that lured him from the seemingly inevitable but "unwelcome bed" of full ordination. His passionate affection for the young Ellen Terry, which seems to have been a more profound devotion than George Bernard Shaw's would be in the actress' middle age, his intensifying obsession with child actresses in general in his later years, his infusion of theatricality even into his photographs of non-actresses—all suggest that the mobile self-definition of acting crystallized the potential power he found in the little girl. His photographic allegiance to the performing self suggested a commitment to the metamorphic mystery of personality which few artists, then and now, are brave enough to pledge. His 16 July 1887 letter to the *St. James Gazette,* defending the good health and high spirits of stage children, evokes the vitalism acting epitomized. After describing "the vigor of *life*" in three stage children who accompanied him to Brighton, he concludes: "A taste for *acting* is one of the strongest passions of human nature. . . . Stage children show it almost from infancy

. . . they simply rejoiced in their work 'even as a giant to run his course.' "[13]

The inexhaustible gusto and intensity of these three young actresses embody the lure of the Carrollian little girl. The poignance of her fleeting performance is a protest against an adulthood that robs her not of innocence or chastity, but of vitality. In *Literary Women,* Ellen Moers finds a similar protest in the poems of Christina Rossetti and in Emily Brontë's *Wuthering Heights* against an adulthood that censors the intense erotic violence permitted to little girls.[14] The erotic excitement one can hardly deny in Carroll's love for his girl children may find one source in the eroticism female childhood sanctioned. Some such emotion seems to underlie his admission to Gertrude Thomson: "I confess I do *not* admire naked *boys,* in pictures. They always seem to me to need *clothes:* whereas one hardly sees why the lovely forms of girls should *ever* be covered up!"[15] Could Carroll have sensed that to "cover up" a girl in the panoply of womanhood is to smother a wealth of erotic energy, while to "cover up" a boy in the uniforms of manhood is to sanction and to symbolize childhood's aggressive vitalism?

Carroll's faith in performing little girls was a virtually unique tribute, a denial of the shrouded langour so many Victorians wanted women and children to embody. His use of props to define and set off the sitters in his photographs is a familiar device in Victorian visual art, particularly in its representations of women and girls, but Carroll uses props in bold and striking fashion. Perhaps nineteenth-century artists sensed that the power of women was so overwhelming, but officially so undefined, that they relied on properties less as pure decoration than as foils, defining obliquely what woman was and was not; the foils claim to explain the mystery of womanhood, but more often than not they intensify it. We remember Alice's subtle relation to the pig in Tenniel's illustration, where the pig functions as the navel both of the composition and of Alice's body: at the same time as it completes the circle she makes, her imperious purity both eschews and acknowledges its implication of her. In the same way, Victorian art uses foils and contrasts both to intensify the suggestive potential of women and girls and to exorcise the unnamed disturbances they arouse.

So, in later, sentimental illustrations, Alice is kept chastely remote from the creatures of Wonderland. (See Figure 4.) Though her inces-

[13]Quoted in Lennon, pp. 245-246.
[14]Ellen Moers, *Literary Women* (New York: Doubleday & Co., Inc., 1976), pp. 99-107.
[15]February 27, 1893; *The Letters of Lewis Carroll,* ed. Morton Cohen, 2 vols. (New York: Oxford University Press, 1979), II: 947.

sant question in the novel—her recurrent, plaintive "who am I?"—suggests the fluid boundaries between Alice and the creatures of her dream, these illustrations exorcise Carroll's disturbing suggestions: his dynamic fallen child, taking to herself the monsters and monstrosities of Wonderland, becomes a coolly immunized traveler. Unlike Ten-

Figure 4. Arthur Rackham, from *Alice's Adventures in Wonderland*.

56

niel's pig drawing, Rackham's charming illustration acts in this reassuringly sentimental way: its contrasts dispel our fears for the preservation of Alice's identity. The mushroom's forbidding head, and her own inquisitive distance, push her back from the Caterpillar; the straight light line of her body aligns her compositionally with the neutrality of the mushrooms' stems, not with the Caterpillar's sinuous dark grotesquerie. The monster as foil reassures us of the little girl's purity.

These various ways of juxtaposing Alice with the monsters she dreams exemplify the tensions Victorian artists perceived between Beauty and the Beast, two perennial types in their art. Generally, the artist wants to shield Beauty against contamination by her hybrid interlocutor, but in some representations, his alienation from humanity mirrors her own. Walter Crane's elegant illustration of the fairy tale, where Beauty and Beast sit facing each other on a drawing-room sofa, holds these dual possibilities in suspension. (See Figure 5.) The monster is defined by compositional aggression, leaning toward the woman's self-enclosed sphere while she shrinks delicately away. Nevertheless, there are witty subterranean hints of an alliance between Beauty and Beast, or at least of a certain droll bestiality in the woman that makes this picture more subtle and sophisticated than most Victorian foil paintings. In a visual symphony of pink and red, Beauty and the Beast wear complementary colors, the red slashes in Beauty's dress, her hair, and her fan seeming to beckon toward the Beast's blatant red waistcoat and hooves. Moreover, though her diminutive red feet are tucked demurely under her dress, her skirt extends out to meet the Beast's cloven hooves and to echo their shape. The Beast does not exorcise, but arouses, his counterpoint within Beauty; Crane's foil

Figure 5. Walter Crane, illustration of "Beauty and the Beast."

whispers to us the happy hint that a lady can survive in a drawing room with gently cloven feet. The hint of kinship in Crane's illustration reminds us of *Alice* in its covert, affectionate complicity between the female's politeness and the monster's assault, a complicity that still arouses us in the charged confrontations of woman and monster

Figure 6. Arthur Hughes, illustration of Christina Rossetti's *Speaking Likenesses*.

in such popular films as *King Kong* and *Alien,* whose women and monsters converge within a male-controlled and maddened world.

In some of the most interestingly savage Victorian children's books, this interchangeability of Beauty and Beast is a central theme. (See Figure 6.) In Christina Rossetti's *Speaking Likenesses,* illustrated here by Arthur Hughes, an angry little girl dreams of a birthday party invaded by monstrous, anarchic creatures, over which she herself presides in the guise of a furious Queen. In Hughes' illustration, Lewis Carroll's symbolism becomes explosively explicit: though the helpless little girl at the center of the composition is as boneless, pure, and inexpressive as we would expect, monsters form themselves from the planes and contours of her body, her very malleability giving shape to weird personifications of misrule. Like the mad Queens in the *Alices,* Hughes' doppelgänger Queen is a dream of suppressed female fury whose monstrosity is the foundation of her power. The composition of this mad birthday party allows no doubt that the energy of monsters inheres in a little girl's graceful attitudes, monsters who (in a dream at least) become the agents of rule. The foils no longer insulate the female from contamination, but fuel a nightmare of her latent power.

Hughes' illustration of Christina Rossetti's vision is safely tucked away within the framework of a moralistic children's book in which, upon the little girl's awakening, her dream of power reduces itself to a dream of terror. Similarly, in Lewis Carroll's dream books, an acknowledged influence on Christina Rossetti's, the complexities of the little girl's dream decompose into idyllic wonderment when she awakes. But within the confines of fantasy or dream, the pure female reveals latent and powerful incarnations. When these dreams are illustrated, their sharply contoured symbolism does not dispel itself into golden memories or cautionary morals; a richly conceived foil like Alice's pig expands the reader's easy formulations about the purity of women and girls, eliciting the boundless potential within polite female respectability, defining not what the little girl is exempt from, but what she might become. The popularity of fairy photographs in late Victorian England, in which a bourgeois, beribboned little girl is often posed with a supposedly authentic flying fairy, epitomizes the child's potential for transformation and flight. The subversive import of *Beauty and the Beast* galvanizes the sharp contrasts of Victorian melodrama: Dickens' manic, misshapen Quilp, for example, lends forbidden energy to his stern Little Nell, while Christina Rossetti's Laura and Lizzie in *Goblin Market* must amputate their own irresistible potential toward becoming goblins themselves. Gothic literature, too, whispers of these forbidden transformations. In "The Lifted

Veil,'' George Eliot's Gothic tale, a proper heroine becomes a lamia when seen truly, and a female corpse is suddenly galvanized into enraged life; the vampirized women in Bram Stoker's *Dracula* outdo their diabolical Master in virtuoso self-transformations, peregrinations, and flights of perception. Even Tenniel's well-known illustration of Carroll's ''Jabberwocky'' presents a long-haired youth, who shown from behind looks suspiciously like Alice, facing a horrible swooping monster that suggests a looking-glass self. The best-known interchange between Beauty and Beast in Victorian literature may come from *Wuthering Heights,* when the pure, sheltered heroine plaintively evokes her goblin self with the cry, ''I *am* Heathcliff.'' The very emphasis in Victorian iconography on female placidity and passivity, on exemption from mobile and passionate energy, expands into dreams of metamorphosis, transcendence, and redemptive monstrosity.

It is in this context of iconographic examination of female nature that the fascination of Lewis Carroll's Alice becomes clear. The little girl alone is free to dream, to grow, to metamorphose; she is a pristine but safely guarded vehicle of female power. In Carroll's own illustrations and photographs, though, the affinity between Beauty and Beast lacks intimacy; monsters do not form themselves from the contours of her body; the secret interchange between child and creature generates not so much mutuality as vertigo. Alice's relation to the Victorian type of the fallen woman extends beyond the simple fact of her fall and the powers it bestows on her to create and destroy worlds: like her adult counterparts in literature and art, Alice is a ''fabulous monster'' of solitude, nibbling at the identities of the creatures she encounters without disappearing into them. Alice shares with her dream-creatures their mobility, their obsessions, but like the fallen woman, that aloof and outcast pariah, she refrains from embracing them.

Part of the intensity of the *Alice* books comes from this perpetual tension between intimacy and estrangement. (See Figure 7.) Lewis Carroll's own drawing of Alice and the Rabbit exemplifies the simultaneous power of relationship and revulsion. The mesmeric intensity of Alice's gaze, and the Rabbit's taut awareness of it, is far more suggestive than the ceremonial indifference Rackham depicts between Alice and the Caterpiller. Alice and the Rabbit are welded to each other by the power of their gaze, though there remains an electric distance between looker and object.

More disturbing still, unlike his subsequent illustrators, Carroll divides the focus of the drawing so that Alice is not central to it: we initially see neither Alice nor the Rabbit, but the significant No-Man's-Land between them. This is not an illustration of a remote child spectator, but of the complex relationship between Alice and her creature. Carroll compounds this emphasis on interrelationship by drawing the picture to the scale of the Rabbit, rather than using Alice as scale, so that we see with him Alice looming toward him, a curious prophecy of the "fabulous monster" the *Looking-Glass* Unicorn will discover when he sees her, or even of the looming Jabberwocky itself. A rabbit in a frock-coat becomes our norm of size, a demure little girl our looming monster: identities here are so bewildered between Beauty and Beast that the viewer can do nothing but circle back and forth between them. No later illustrator dared let a figure other than Alice provide the scale of an illustration. Only the author himself deprives us of our norms by providing this final turn of the screw, stripping his beloved child of her last human immunity from the world she both dreams and becomes.

The dream license with which Carroll allowed Alice to assume the perversities of the fallen woman and the distortions of the monster represents either a mad assault on or a profound appreciation of the

Figure 7. Lewis Carroll, from *Alice's Adventures Under Ground.*

integrity of female childhood; our perspective depends upon who we are. By now, we have all had to learn that within the "golden afternoon" of Wonderland lie dark books indeed, rife with anxiety and aggression, the agony of forgetting countered only by the agony of memory.[16] Freudian critics have bequeathed to us the specter of Lewis Carroll as himself the perverse monster, brandishing pen and camera as he looms over the pure little girl to violate her: the main impact of the Freudian vogue of the 1930s was a feeling that innocent children should be saved from the *Alice* books. A demonic *Alice* has lurked in the wings for a long time, shadowing and titillating our appreciation of this paean to the purity of little girlhood.

Now that Morton N. Cohen has published replicas of some of Carroll's notorious nude photographs, the idea of which has shocked our own century far more than it did the Victorians, the possibly demonic and perverse Carroll surfaces in our minds once more.[17] Questions tease us about the ultimate direction of his verbal and visual celebrations of little girls: are they a violation of childhood, however voyeuristic and oblique, or is Carroll the purest Arnoldian critic of female children, appreciating the object as in itself it really is, adopting the camera's loving detachment in order to define its subject's value to the world? Feminist viewers might find themselves particularly perplexed by Carroll's obsessive celebration of girlhood, uncertain whether his worship violates his subject or comprehends it.

Answers to these oracular questions suggest themselves only in pictures. Consider a particularly innocent one of still another Alice, Alice Price. (See Figure 8.) As opposed to the monstrous Alice who gazed somewhat hungrily at a white rabbit, Alice Price is the center of a pristinely sentimental Victorian tableau, a little girl with her doll, radiating exemplary femininity, contented domesticity, and future motherhood. But the more we look at this apparent emblem of feminine virtue, the more we see it grow into suggestions of monstrosity. The pensive sensuality of the child's pose, the erotic hunger of her expression, become more apparent to us as we look, until the doll becomes less a thing to nourish than a thing to eat. This suggestive gem of a photo subtly mocks proper little motherhood by supplying a mobile child with a foil as rich in contradictory implications as Tenniel's pig. The discreetly carnivorous rapture with which Alice eyes her doll will suffuse the expression of a later Victorian child gazing at a different sort of doll: Aubrey Beardsley's elegantly ravenous Salomé

[16]*Aspects of Alice* is a symphony of dark *Alices*. For a moving account of their dependence on memory, see Lionel Morton, "Memory in the *Alice* Books," *Nineteenth-Century Fiction* 33 (Dec. 1978), 285-308.

[17]See Morton Cohen, *Lewis Carroll, Photographer of Children: Four Nude Studies* (New York: Clarkson N. Potter, 1979).

as she leans forward to kiss the dead lips of John the Baptist. In Beardsley's fin-de-siècle variant of a familiar Victorian motif, the foil appropriates all the picture's purity, the little girl all its monstrous lust. Carroll's photograph is content to whisper the possibility of this inversion, hinting at an uneasy rapport between the domestic and the demonic as they threaten to merge altogether. Softly loving Alice Price grows into another manifestation of the hungry Alice we know, an uncontained pioneer whose "deepest impulses [involve] power and aggression."[18]

[18]Kincaid, 95.

Figure 8. Lewis Carroll, photograph of Alice Price and doll.

Carroll's extraordinary tact as an artist infuses acceptable little girls with an energy that was in itself unacceptable. Despite his safe life, his career tiptoes along the dangerous line that separates coziness from unease. The explosive potential he sensed in his dream-children is a pervasive but unspoken awareness in Victorian iconography, where the line between sentimentality and perversity stretches so thin as to be at times invisible. Redemptive love itself becomes a dangerous issue, though love was the only emotional activity most readers found acceptable in women. Its holy influence was supposed to defuse the self, its hungers, its ambitions, its energy, its drive for power. Yet, in fin-de-siècle literature particularly, love threatens to become a new, and dangerous, source of power in itself. Hardy's Tess falls in love and finds gratification through murder; Wilde's Salomé falls in love and creates a murder that is a triumph of perverse aestheticism. Throughout the century, the popular icon of the fallen woman fuels with forbidden love a drive for power Victorian society taboos in women. The blessed emotion that was supposed to obliterate women becomes an illicit source of female strength. This tortured perception of the mixed potential of women in love finds one culmination in D. H. Lawrence's great novel of that name, whose Ursula and Gudrun seem to promise the solace of repose, but whose love is underlain by their lethal, and irrepressible, energy.

The power and erotic energy within a dream of purity all inhere in the mutable little girls Carroll immortalized. (See Figure 9). His photographs of nude children need no metaphorical foils to define their powers: they are simply the objects themselves. Some embarrassed viewers have tried to see no sexuality in these photographs, but it seems to me needlessly apologetic to deny the eroticism of this

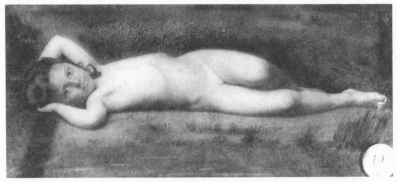

Figure 9. Lewis Carroll, photograph of Evelyn Hatch. Reproduced courtesy of the Rosenbach Foundation and by permission of the Charles L. Dodgson Estate, A. P. Watt, Ltd.

beautiful little odalisque. Since her sexuality is not imaged forth in foils, emblems, or metaphors, Carroll's Evelyn Hatch seems to me a far more healthily realized figure than Beardsley's Salomé, who needs the Baptist's purity to define her lust, or even than Nabokov's sado-masochistic dream of Lolita, for Evelyn Hatch is allowed to be at one with her own implied powers. Thus, the achievement of this photograph lies in its pure acceptance of what Carroll's Victorian contemporaries perceived as demonic and dangerous. Unlike Alice, Evelyn Hatch needs no creatures to inform us that she is both animal and dreamer, pig and pure little girl. Carroll as camera eye does perfect justice to the self-transforming mobility of his model. The eroticism, along with the passionate and seditious powers this had come to imply, belongs to the child; the artist merely understands it. Though he spoke a halting, cryptic language, Lewis Carroll recognized the fallen woman's metamorphic complexity within an unfallen child on a golden afternoon. As an infallibly courteous Victorian gentleman, he granted Alice and the rest of his child-friends the powers that were theirs.

CARROLL'S WELL-VERSED NARRATIVE:
THROUGH THE LOOKING-GLASS

Beverly Lyon Clark

> *You say that I'm "to write a verse"—*
> *O Maggie, put it quite*
> *The other way, and kindly say*
> *That I'm "averse to write"!*[1]

In writing to his child-friends Lewis Carroll was not averse to verse, however he might tease. Nor was he averse in his fiction—for it comprises one of the most memorable features of his *Alice* books. It contributes to the humor and nonsense and absurdity of the books, through its play with "real"-world forms and its parody, and through its concreteness and its interaction with the surrounding prose.

Carroll played with "real"-world forms sometimes by making things more orderly and sometimes by making them less. But of course order and disorder are all a matter of perspective. When Humpty Dumpty defines glory as "a nice knock-down argument" he disorders our real-world semantic order, from one perspective, but the simple act of defining the word, of associating it with a meaning and not leaving it in the limbo of meaningless noises, is itself an act of order. Humpty Dumpty's new order may be unfamiliar, but it is not entirely chaotic. Or take "Jabberwocky." Does it disorder our orderly universe? Yes, in part, for "brillig" and "slithy" have no familiar meaning. Yet, as students of language are fond of pointing out, the grammatical structure of the poem is orderly, making it possible for us to decipher, for instance, the parts of speech to which the nonsense words belong. And the words themselves combine consonants and vowels the way English words do (unlike, say, the Wonderland Gryphon's "Hjckrrh!"). Further, Humpty Dumpty's explication provides an ordering of the meaning as well. When he expounds, " '*Brillig*' means four o'clock in the afternoon—the time when you begin *broiling* things for dinner,"[2] he describes a world with a modicum of order, one that can be envisioned as in, say, Tenniel's drawing.

---

[1] Letter to Margaret Cunnynghame, 10 April 1871, *The Letters of Lewis Carroll,* ed. Morton N. Cohen, with the assistance of Roger Lancelyn Green, Vol. 1 (New York: Oxford Univ. Press, 1979), p. 163. Other references to letters are given parenthetically in the text, preceded by the word "*Letters.*"

[2] *Alice in Wonderland: Authoritative Texts of* Alice's Adventures in Wonderland, Through the Looking-Glass, The Hunting of the Snark, *Backgrounds, Essays in Criticism,* ed. Donald J. Gray (New York: Norton, 1971), p. 164. All parenthetical page references not otherwise labeled are to this volume. All italics are Carroll's.

Another way of describing Carroll's play with "real"-world forms is in terms of open and closed fields. Susan Stewart, in her recent study *Nonsense,* catalogues nonsense transformations and finds some within the closed fields described by Elizabeth Sewell in her early *Field of Nonsense,* closing what is traditionally open, while others do the inverse, opening what is closed. Yet whatever we call the two transformations—whether we use this broad definition or else associate nonsense only with the first kind of transformation and associate the second with the absurd—Carroll uses both kinds. He sometimes opens what is traditionally closed (making a mirror into a door) and sometimes closes what is traditionally open and on-going (making time stand still at six o'clock). And often what Carroll does is a complex amalgam of both opening and closing. In his parodies, for instance, some of the wordplay focuses attention on the words, fencing them off from reality, making them a closed world: rhyme and alliteration draw attention to the words and distract us from whatever it is the words are meant to refer to. The parodies also close themselves off as separate worlds to the extent that they do not refer to recognizable reality: how does one balance anything as slippery and floppy as an eel on the end of one's nose? On the other hand, the references to artifacts outside the poems—to other poems—opens the form, and the parodies would also seem to shatter the closed universes of the pietistic poems they mock. The parodies operate in both closed and open fields—they both order and disorder—and part of their effect derives from the confrontation between the two. We can call them nonsense, or something else, but the parodies draw upon both kinds of transformation.

It has become convenient to refer offhand to most of the verse in the *Alice* books as parodies. But again we run into a problem of definition. This time I want to define the term more narrowly, for the very general way in which we use "parody" sometimes blinds us to important distinctions. Sometimes we call something a parody if it reminds us of a previous work, whether or not any satire is intended. But I'd like to reserve parody for something that satirizes. Dwight Macdonald, for instance, situates Carroll's works closer to what he calls burlesque than to parody: "he simply injected an absurd content into the original form with no intention of literary criticism." Macdonald is right for some of Carroll's verse, but I would disagree with his contention that Carroll never intended literary criticism, for sometimes Carroll does intend literary, if not moral, criticism.[3]

[3]*Parodies: An Anthology from Chaucer to Beerbohm—and After,* ed. Dwight Macdonald (New York: Random House, 1960), p. 278. I would also disagree somewhat with Martin Gardner, who, in "Speak Roughly," in *Lewis Carroll Observed: A Collection*

Sometimes, if not always. For only in *Alice's Adventures in Wonderland* is the verse truly parodic. *"How doth the little crocodile,"* for instance, undermines the pious preaching of Isaac Watts's "How doth the little busy bee," which admonishes children to keep busy and avoid mischief: the crocodile presented for our emulation, far from skillfully building a cell or neatly spreading wax, "cheerfully" and "neatly" and "gently"—snares fishes. Much of the other pious verse that Carroll parodies in *Wonderland* is similarly subverted. While Carroll does not entirely disagree with the sentiments of the poems he parodies—especially in later life, when he wanted to outbowdlerize Bowdler—and thus does not mock that which is preached, he does mock the preaching. Carroll may not be criticizing the content (he surely is not inciting children to be slothful), but he does criticize the literary purpose of didactic verse, the way in which it tried to control children. In part Carroll may simply be entering into the child's perspective, adopting the child's responses to pietistic verse, for he shows considerable sympathy for the child's point of view. And perhaps Carroll's satire of the didacticism of previous children's literature clears a niche for the new kind of children's literature he wanted to write. Much as Alice tries to define herself by attempting to recite familiar verse, Carroll seems, intentionally or not, to be defining his fiction through Alice's failure to define herself, through her mangling of her recitations.

In *Through the Looking-Glass,* however, it is as if Carroll's success with his first children's book freed him from the need to comment on what previous writers had done for, or to, children. The verse is less parodic. Although some of it plays with pre-existing poems, it is harder to label such playing parody, harder to convict it of literary criticism. Carroll's "parodies" in the two books might be placed on a continuum, from the true parodies like that of Watts to reflections of the original that are not necessarily satires (what Macdonald describes), to mere echoes that may not actually be related to a so-called original. The drinking song begot of Scott, sung at the Looking-glass banquet, mimics some lines of the original but probably without any intent to satirize. And still farther from parody is "The Walrus and the Carpenter," which shares its meter and rhyme scheme with

---

of Unpublished Photographs, Drawings, Poetry, and New Essays, ed. Edward Guiliano (New York: Clarkson N. Potter, 1976), p. 20, claims that Carroll does not "copy the style of a poet" for purposes of literary criticism (here seconding Macdonald), and implies that Carroll does not intend "to deflate the pious, pompous, and hypocritical morality of Victorian times" but rather was an exponent of such morality. Donald Rackin seems closer to the truth when he finds "a satirical hit at the didactic, moralistic manner of the bulk of nineteenth-century children's literature" ("Corrective Laughter: Carroll's *Alice* and Popular Children's Literature of the Nineteenth Century," *Journal of Popular Culture,* 1 [1967], 244).

Thomas Hood's "The Dream of Eugene Aram" and also the discovery of an unexpected murderer, but which is not otherwise tied to the so-called original. Carroll himself wrote in a letter to his uncle, "I had no particular poem in mind. The metre is a common one, and I don't think 'Eugene Aram' suggested it more than the many other poems I have read in the same metre" (*Letters,* p. 177).

Looking-Glass verse tends toward this latter end of the continuum. Carroll here does not demolish children's verse. For the most part, he either uses fantastical nursery rhymes, which do not need to be demolished, or else he plays with adult poetry, which can perhaps be poked and prodded at but need not be so utterly crushed as the sugar-coated moralizing intended for children.

I will demonstrate how Carroll uses pre-existing verse in *Looking-Glass* by examining the changes he rings on Wordsworth's "Resolution and Independence." The White Knight's poem includes echoes of other poems—Wordsworth's "The Thorn" and Thomas Moore's "My Heart and Lute"—but I'll concentrate on "Resolution and Independence." Carroll had written an early version of his poem by 1856, and this version describes a situation fairly close to that in Wordsworth's poem: in both the narrator encounters an extremely old man upon the moor, asks his occupation, and is comforted by the exchange—although Wordsworth's narrator is comforted by the man's cheer and steadfastness, while Carroll's is comforted by the man's "kind intent / To drink my health in beer" (p. 250). The closest verbal echoes are in the closing lines. Wordsworth ends with "I'll think of the Leech-gatherer on the lonely moor!",[4] and Carroll ends with "I think of that strange wanderer / Upon the lonely moor."

This echoing of concluding lines is emblematic of the relationship between the two poems. While the Watts parody starts off proclaiming the poem it twists, repeating the opening "How doth the little," as well as "Improve" and "shining" in the second line, the Wordsworth derivative waits till the conclusion for a close verbal echo. Furthermore, Carroll entirely omits all reference to the meditative early verses of Wordsworth's poem, and even changes the meter and rhyme scheme. "Upon the Lonely Moor" is simply not very close to "Resolution and Independence." And it is not that Wordsworth's lines utterly forbid parody. Surely, if he had wanted to, Carroll could have embellished "Such seemed this Man, not all alive nor dead, / Nor all asleep" by adding something like (but better than) "Nor scrubbing scones nor eating flies / Nor starting in to weep." He

---

[4] *The Prelude; with a Selection from the Shorter Poems, the Sonnets,* The Recluse, *and* The Excursion; *and Three Essays on the Art of Poetry,* ed. and introd. Carlos Baker (1954; rpt. New York: Holt, Rinehart and Winston, 1966), p. 141.

apparently wanted to use Wordsworth's dramatic situation as a scaffolding more than he wanted to use Wordsworth's poem as a source
for parody.

The later version of Carroll's poem, the one that appears in
Looking-Glass, is even farther from Wordsworth. The echo in the last
two lines has entirely disappeared, and so has all reference to moors.
Instead of situating his aged man on a romantic and evocative moor
Carroll sits him on a gate. Compared to the earlier version, the
nonsense is better, the parody less.

Nevertheless, Carroll himself did call the poem a parody, in a letter
to his uncle—but he went on to modify his use of the term: " 'Sitting
on a Gate' *is* a parody, though not as to style or metre—but its plot is
borrowed from Wordsworth's 'Resolution and Independence' . . ."
(*Letters,* p. 177). Carroll uses the term "parody" for lack of a better
word, to describe his borrowing of the plot, or dramatic situation, his
use of the poem as a scaffolding. He goes on to indicate what in
Wordsworth's poem he might well like to satirize, for it is "a poem
that has always amused me a good deal (though it is by no means a
comic poem) by the absurd way in which the poet goes on questioning
the poor old leech-gatherer, making him tell his history over and over
again, and never attending to what he says. Wordsworth ends with a
moral—an example I have *not* followed." Carroll uses Wordsworth's
dramatic situation here, but doing so, though it may poke fun at the
narrator's greater interest in his own thoughts than in human interaction, does not undermine Wordsworth's sentiments, his praise of
resolution, nor his communing with nature, nor his introspection.
And the final version of the poem has strayed far enough from the
original that Carroll needs to stress to his uncle that it *is* a parody.

We may be too eager to find satiric comment on Wordsworth in
Carroll's poem, since the convenient label for the poem is parody and
that is what parody is supposed to do. But while Carroll might not
mind tweaking Wordsworth's nose when he starts platitudinizing,
Carroll less clearly satirizes Wordsworth than he does Watts in the
crocodile poem. And in other derived poems in *Looking-Glass,* such
as that sired by Scott, the original neither pedantic nor moralistic, it is
even harder to find what Carroll could be satirizing. The complexity
of the relationship between Carroll's and Wordsworth's poems, or
Carroll's and Scott's, a relationship not easily defined by our usual interpretation of "parody," complements the complexity of Carroll's
nonsense and absurdity, which both reveres and defies, both orders
and disorders, both closes and opens.

Another way in which Carroll's verse is humorous and nonsensical,
in addition to parodying and playing with forms from the "real"

world, is through what Elizabeth Sewell calls "a careful addiction to the concrete."[5] Instead of evoking a twinkling star and comparing it to a diamond, Carroll makes a bat twinkle like a tea-tray. Or he unites shoes, ships and sealing wax, or cabbages and kings. Yet not all of Carroll's verse is humorous in precisely this way. Some of it is less concrete and complete in itself, and part of its humor lies in how it integrates with the surrounding narrative. And since little or no attention has been paid to this other source of humor, I am going to concentrate on it at the expense of "careful concreteness." Again, as with the parodic playing with form, the humor derives from a varying tension, or confrontation, between opening and closing the verse: the concreteness and completeness tend to close it, while the integration with the narrative opens it. In *Wonderland* the King of Hearts attempts to integrate verse into the story when he uses the lines beginning *"They told me you had been to her"* as evidence of the Knave's guilt. Yet the ambiguous pronoun references in the lines invite all interpretations—and substantiate none. And the King's attempt to use this verse as evidence ironically substantiates its inadmissibility and hence underscores the disjunction between verse and story. Much of the humor of the verse derives from the use the King makes of it.

Looking-Glass verse tends to be even more integrated with the narrative. Both form and content are integrated, the latter in four ways. I will first discuss the integration of the content, and then turn to the form.

Overall, the content integrates with the prose thematically. Alice finally says, with only slight exaggeration, that the poetry was "all about fishes" (p. 208). (And in the context of playing with kittens, and frequently thinking about eating, it is not amiss to dream about fishes.) In addition, some of the verse relates directly to the action: the Red Queen sings a lullaby when the White Queen wants to nap; and the creatures sing toasts at the closing banquet.[6] Some of the verse is interpreted by the characters, who thereby attempt, as it were, to accommodate the verse to the narrative: Humpty Dumpty interprets "Jabberwocky"; and even the Tweedles offer some interpretations of "The Walrus and the Carpenter." Finally, some of the verse is enacted in the story: notably, the nursery rhymes come to life.

In providing sources for Looking-glass characters, the nursery rhymes strengthen the integration of verse and story. Much as Wonderland creatures sprout from metaphoric proverbs (except for

---

[5] *The Field of Nonsense* (London: Chatto and Windus, 1952), p. 58.

[6] The verse in the episode that Carroll finally omitted from *Looking-Glass,* that of the Wasp in a Wig, likewise relates to the action, for the Wasp tells how he came to wear a wig.

the Queen of Hearts and company, derived in part from a nursery rhyme but also from playing cards), such Looking-glass creatures as Humpty Dumpty and the Tweedles derive from nursery rhymes. As Roger Henkle notes, the careers of the nursery-rhyme creatures "are predetermined by the nursery rhymes about them"[7]—they derive, in other words, from entire verse-stories, not from mere phrases. Or, even if the creatures are ignorant of their predetermining verses, Alice and the reader are not, and we see how the verse does indeed determine actions, how highly integrated verse and narrative are. In *Wonderland,* on the other hand, while the King acts as if the previous behavior of the Knave of Hearts has been described by a nursery rhyme, Alice and the reader are not convinced. The nursery rhyme does not have determining force there—it is merely posited—while nursery rhymes do affect Looking-glass world, the verse does affect the narrative: Humpty Dumpty does come crashing down.

The appearance of nursery-rhyme characters in *Looking-Glass* also makes the book self-conscious because Alice knows about the characters in the story of her adventures through knowing other stories—she is "in the ambiguous position of being a reader in a story where she meets fictitious characters and so knows all about them."[8] This self-consciousness is somewhat different from self-consciousness in *Wonderland.* There Alice may comment that the Mouse has reached the fifth bend of his concrete poem, self-consciously commenting on the poem; but it is only the poem that she views as a literary artifact, not the creatures she encounters. Her comments underline the differences between the poem and the narrative rather than merge them. In *Looking-Glass,* though, she is self-conscious about both poems and narrative, and she even wonders if she herself is part of the Red King's dream. Although Alice may simply be playing another version of "Let's pretend" at the end, when she asks Kitty which dreamed it, her question does hint at a serious issue. And the poem that concludes *Looking-Glass,* ending as it does with *"Life, what is it but a dream?"* (p. 209), continues the impetus of self-consciousness. Such self-consciousness can at first remind the reader of the boundaries between fiction and reality, since the fiction proclaims its fictionality. Hence it would close the work off from reality. Yet, as Borges queries of the work within a work: "Why does it disquiet us to know that Don Quixote is a reader of the *Quixote,* and Hamlet is a spectator of *Hamlet*? I believe I have found the answer: those inversions suggest that if the characters in a story can be readers

---

[7]"The Mad Hatter's World," *Virginia Quarterly Review,* 49 (1973), 108.
[8]Barbara Hardy, "Fantasy and Dream," in *Tellers and Listeners: The Narrative Imagination* (London: Athlone, 1975), p. 40.

or spectators, then we, their readers or spectators, can be fictitious."[9] The self-consciousness in *Looking-Glass* likewise hints that what appears tangible may be only a dream, that presumed realities are really fantasies, that reality is subjective. *Looking-Glass* may not be a fully self-conscious novel, one that, in Robert Alter's words, "systematically flaunts its own condition of artifice and . . . by so doing probes into the problematic relationship between real-seeming artifice and reality,"[10] but it does tend somewhat in that direction, to confound reality and fiction. Once again, though indirectly, the *Looking-Glass* verse occasions integration, integration here of the larger realms of fiction and reality. And once again, *Looking-Glass* balances closure and self-containment with openness and permeation.

Enough of metaphysics and back to the verse again: not only is the content integrated with the narrative but so is the form. Not only is there thematic continuity between verse and prose, via fishes, and not only is one sometimes an adumbration of the other—as with the Tweedles, Humpty Dumpty, and the Lion and the Unicorn—but the physical integration of the two has also increased in *Looking-Glass.* Of course, this verse, like the verse in *Wonderland,* is set off from the rest of the text by being in verse form. Yet in *Looking-Glass* the segregation of verse and prose falters. Perhaps even the railway passengers' refrain, " ——— is worth a thousand ——— a ———," is a verse more completely integrated with narrative, a verse not typographically segregated: Alice considers the refrain "like the chorus of a song" (p. 129).

Once more I would like to amplify the argument by examining specific examples. First I will look at the White Knight's verse and then Humpty Dumpty's, both of which merge with the surrounding narrative.

After droning on *"mumblingly and low"* with his *"so"/"know"/ "slow"* rhymes, the White Knight abruptly ends his poem with *"A-sitting on a gate"* (p. 190). The last line provides the rhyme for "weight" so long held in abeyance, until the record needle finally came unstuck, and hence provides some closure. Yet the poem shows a tendency to continue into, merge with, the ensuing narrative. For the interminable o-rhymes, essentially paratactic, could go on forever, comic invention willing. And they make the abrupt concluding line seem tacked on, anticlimactic. This anticlimax is humorous, as Carroll wants it to be, but it also, as Barbara Herrnstein Smith might note,

[9] "Partial Enchantments of the *Quixote,"* in *Other Inquisitions, 1937-1952,* trans. Ruth L. C. Simms, introd. James Irby (Austin: Univ. of Texas Press, 1964), p. 46.
[10] *Partial Magic: The Novel as a Self-Conscious Genre* (Berkeley: Univ. of California Press, 1975), p. x.

leaves the reader "with residual expectations."[11] These residual expectations make the reader receptive to the possibility of an additional line or lines. And, in fact, the next words the White Knight speaks are "You've only a few yards to go"—consistent with the poem's meter and rhyme. The poem pushes beyond its physical boundaries.

Humpty Dumpty's verse likewise shows a tendency to continue into the narrative, a merging anticipated by Alice's frequent interruptions during the recitation. Some of the stanzas are as follows:

> The little fishes' answer was
> 'We cannot do it, Sir, because————'
> . . .
> And he was very proud and stiff:
> He said 'I'd go and wake them, if————'
> . . .
> And when I found the door was shut,
> I tried to turn the handle, but————
>
> (pp. 167-168)

Alice's comment shortly after hearing the poem, as she leaves Humpty Dumpty, is "of all the unsatisfactory people I *ever* met————." Because of forces working against closure in the poem, her comment would seem to be a reprise of the unfinished sentences in the above stanzas.

Now it is not that there are no forces working to close the poem. The line that Alice speaks and that could continue the poem is not spoken immediately after Humpty Dumpty's recitation, nor is it spoken by the character reciting the poem, nor is it a complete couplet, nor is it metrically consistent with the poem. Then, too, we may resolve some of the poem's lack of closure by declaring it humorous, labeling its dissonance and making it acceptable, so that we need not continue to seek closure. Yet the forces working against closure are stronger.

In the first place, the verse purports to tell a narrative, but its story is truncated. The narrator tells of the need to wake the little fishes and of going to the locked door and trying to get through. We expect some kind of resolution: perhaps the narrator breaks through the door, perhaps the door proves sentient and assaults the narrator, perhaps the narrator wastes away to a hummingbird egg as he continually pounds and kicks and knocks. Yet the action is not resolved but interrupted. Similarly, we expect resolution of other hints in the plot: what nefarious deed, requiring the presence of the fishes, does the narrator intend to perpetrate with his kettle of water?

[11] Barbara Herrnstein Smith, *Poetic Closure: A Study of How Poems End* (Chicago: Univ. of Chicago Press, 1968), p. 224. I am generally indebted to this lucid discussion of closure.

Instead of resolving the plot the poem simply stops, defying closure. And Alice, puzzled, acts out the reader's discomfort over the poem's abrupt completion. Alice is particularly puzzled by the concluding stanza, the one in which the narrator tries to turn the handle of the door: she pauses, she asks if the poem is over, she finds Humpty Dumpty's dismissal—of the poem and of her—rather sudden. Humpty Dumpty's abrupt good-bye at the end of the poem reinforces the abrupt stopping of the poem itself.

Not only is the narrative action truncated but so too is the sentence begun in the final stanza, as in the other stanzas quoted above. In both the overall plot and also the sentence, the meaning is left hanging: both are semantically incomplete. And the sentence is syntactically incomplete as well.

I can elucidate the syntactic and semantic open-endedness of this verse by comparing it to a rather different open-endedness in verse from *Wonderland.* The verse about the Owl and the Panther concludes thus (in some versions of the poem):

> *When the pie was all finished, the Owl, as a boon,*
> *Was kindly permitted to pocket the spoon:*
> *While the Panther received knife and fork with a growl,*
> *And concluded the banquet by* ————

(pp. 83-84)

The final line is incomplete, but—guided by meter and rhyme, by our knowledge of panthers, by our knowledge that "by" wants here to be followed by a verb ending in "ing"—we can readily complete the line with "eating the Owl." Even the narrative plot of the verse reaches resolution with this ending, thus reinforcing the implicit closure. With our complicity the verse silently reaches syntactic, semantic, and narrative closure. The *Looking-Glass* verse, Humpty Dumpty's open-ended verse, is rather different. The lines are metrically complete, with appropriate end-rhymes, but semantically incomplete. And the narrative plot is incomplete too. Rather like the later riddle poem, " '*First, the fish must be caught,*' " whose riddle is never solved for us, and perhaps a bit like the riddle posed in his own nursery rhyme, Humpty Dumpty's poem reaches no resolution. Although the stanza reaches prosodic closure, thanks to the tidy end rhyme, the meaning stretches beyond the verse form, eluding closure, eluding the tidy solipsizing of the verse.

Much of the humor of Humpty Dumpty's verse derives from its integration with the narrative, its interruptions, its incompleteness. Some critics find this the least satisfactory of Carroll's verse,[12] and

---

[12]See Richard Kelly, *Lewis Carroll* (Boston: Twayne, 1977), p. 71: "This has to be the worst poem in the Alice books. The language is flat and prosaic, the frustrated story line

while it is certainly not the best it does become better if we look at it not in isolation but in context. At times the proper unit of analysis is not the poem by itself but the entire dialogue, of which the poem is just part.

Like Humpty Dumpty's poem, if not always to the same degree, the *Looking-Glass* poems are surprisingly integrated into the story, thematically and even physically. Of course, they remain typographically distinct from the prose as well—and again there is a tension between opening and closing. Another site for this tension is the overall structure of *Looking-Glass*. In fact, the greater merging of poetry and prose, compared to *Wonderland,* may in part compensate for a more rigid, closed structure in *Looking-Glass.* Where *Wonderland* describes a relatively aimless wandering, *Looking-Glass* describes a prescribed progression toward a goal, as Alice moves across the chessboard. The individual chapters reinforce the structure by corresponding to individual squares. Carroll counteracts the rigidity of this structure in several ways. One is his placement of lines of asterisks: in *Wonderland* these asterisks, signalling Alice's changes in size, can appear at the end of a chapter, coinciding with and reinforcing a narrative boundary; in *Looking-Glass,* though, Carroll seems careful not to place asterisks, here signalling movement to the next square, at the end of a chapter. Thus Carroll dissipates, a little, the clear demarcations of his narrative. Similarly, in *Looking-Glass* Carroll sometimes does not complete a sentence begun in one chapter until the following chapter: again, Carroll is ameliorating the strict division into chapters. It is as if he wanted to attenuate the rigid boundaries imposed by the chessboard structure. The greater integration of the verse may be similarly compensatory. It attenuates the rigidities of the external scaffolding of the book, much as narrative plays against and dissipates the external scaffolding of the Ulysses story in *Ulysses.*

In fact, Carroll's integration of verse and narrative in *Looking-Glass* is one of the many ways in which he anticipates twentieth-century literature. In some ways *Wonderland* seems rather modern— as in its associative, non-sequential plotting—and in some ways *Looking-Glass* anticipates current fiction. One such way is the way Carroll incorporates verse. His *Looking-Glass* parodies are not true parodies but rather they play against the scaffolding of pre-existing poems, like some of Yeats's poetry, which uses materials in his *A Vision,* yet the images in, say, the Byzantium poems do not need to be followed back to their source before we can appreciate them. Carroll's

is without interest, the couplets are uninspired and fail to surprise or to delight, and there are almost no true elements of nonsense present, other than in the unstated wish of the narrator and the lack of a conclusion to the work.''

parodies too can stand alone, divorced from their sources. Though not from the narrative. For the relationship between verse and narrative also seems modern. Recent writers like Vladimir Nabokov, Thomas Pynchon, and Robert Coover have incorporated verse in their novels yet subverted strict boundaries. In Nabokov's *Pale Fire,* for instance, the novel's plot grows out of footnotes presumably annotating a poem: the poem is far from a mere set piece that a character happens to recite. These novelists carry further certain hints in Carroll's work, going farther than he in merging verse and narrative, fiction and reality.

The interaction of poem and narrative in *Looking-Glass* may thus be approaching twentieth-century forms of interpenetration. And Carroll's humor derives in part from this integration and in part from the opposing tendency toward concrete completeness. Likewise it derives in part from parody and in part from simply playing with "real"-world forms. The humor and nonsense and absurdity depend on a confrontation between opposites, a confrontation that we cannot quite resolve in "real"-world terms. Defining "glory" as "a nice knock-down argument" disagrees with our usual use of the term. It is hard even to make it agree metaphorically, as we can when glory is described as clouds that we trail as we come from God. Instead, the odd juxtaposition, the unresolved confrontation, makes us laugh, strikes us as absurd. And we resolve the disparity, a little, by calling it nonsense, something that need not overturn our comfortable real world. Yet despite its resolution it still hints at revolution, still hints at a more serious questioning of reality.

THE 1865 *ALICE:*
A NEW APPRAISAL AND A REVISED CENSUS

Selwyn H. Goodacre

The saga of the 1865 *Alice* has long fascinated book collectors the world over, and particularly those of us who specialize in Lewis Carroll. Even those who are unfamiliar with such Carrollian rarieties as *American Telegrams* or *The Alphabet-Cipher* respond to the romantic and extraordinary story of the rejection of the first edition of *Alice's Adventures in Wonderland,* and its subsequent reissue in America as the famed "Appleton Alice." The reasons behind the rejection and the facts behind the whole affair have exercised the minds of many scholars. Many of the answers are known, but even now, all is not totally clear, and the continuing discovery of more copies of the rejected first edition commands a new attention.

I

It is not my intention here to go over yet again the ground that is familiar to most students of Lewis Carroll; nevertheless, if we are to come to some understanding of the matter, certain key facts need to be understood.

The story of *Alice's Adventures* as we now know it is a development of the extempore tale first started on a boat trip on 4 July 1862 for the three daughters of Dean Liddell of Christ Church, Oxford—Lorina, Alice and Edith. The tale was called *Alice's Adventures Under Ground,* and was later extended to almost twice the original length, after several people (including Henry Kingsley and Robinson Duckworth, a member of the original boating trip) had admired the story in its early manuscript form. The book with its new title was printed by the Oxford University Press, published "on commission" by Macmillan for Dodgson, who was therefore responsible for all expenses. The intention was for publication to be in time for a presentation copy to be given to Alice Liddell on 4 July 1865, the anniversary of the river trip. We now need to tread carefully so that we may follow exactly the course of events that occurred.

1. 24 May 1865—Dodgson writes to Macmillan requesting fifty copies to give to his friends, "and the rest of the 2000 you can bind at your leisure and publish at whatever time of the year you think best."[1]

---

[1]Unpublished letter quoted by Morton N. Cohen in "Lewis Carroll and the House of Macmillan," *BIS* 7 (1979), p. 39.

78

2. 25 May 1865—"received copy bound in blank" (*MS Journal*).[2]
3. 27 June 1865—"first copies sent to Macmillan" (*MS Journal*).
4. 15 July 1865 (Sat.)—"Went to Macmillan's, and wrote in 20 or more copies of 'Alice' to go as presents to various friends" (*MS Journal*).
5. 20 July 1865—"Called on Macmillan, and showed him Tenniel's letter about the fairy-tale—he is entirely dissatisfied with the printing of the pictures, and I suppose we shall have to do it all again. (Millais recommends keeping back the two thousand printed at Oxford for a future edition)" (*MS Journal*).
6. 2 August 1865—"Finally decided on the re-print of 'Alice,' and that the first 2000 shall be sold as waste paper. Wrote about it to Macmillan, Combe, and Tenniel" (*MS Journal*).
7. 3 August 1865—(Letter to ? Tom Taylor). "I write to beg that, if you have received the copy I sent you of Alice . . . you will suspend your judgment on it till I can send you a better copy. We are printing it again, as the pictures are so badly done."[3]
8. c. November 1865—letter from Tenniel to Dalziel (the engraver) "I protested so strongly against the disgraceful printing that (Dodgson) *cancelled the edition.*"[4]
9. Date not known—Frederick Macmillan, as reported by S. H. Williams, felt that there was "dissatisfaction with the way the printing was done."[5]

These are the essential documentary records of events.

There have been two major articles on the reasons for the rejection. In "Carroll's Withdrawal of the 1865 *Alice,*" Harry Morgan Ayres tended to concentrate on the defects in the letterpress;[6] for example, he pointed to fourteen "widows," i.e., occurrences of less than a full line at the top of a page; Ayres remarked that the correction of these for the 1866 second edition "on six or seven pages, permitted a better placing of the picture." He could have added that on p. 91, where a line is taken back from p. 92, the outlining of the picture of Alice talking to the Cheshire-Cat is on three sides instead of two, a pleasing ef-

[2]Only 60 percent or so of Dodgson's journal is published in *The Diaries of Lewis Carroll* (London: Cassell, 1953; New York: Oxford Univ. Press, 1954). Citations from unpublished portions of the journals now in the British Library are reproduced courtesy of the C. L. Dodgson Estate and are identified as (*MS Journal*).
[3]*The Letters of Lewis Carroll,* ed. Morton N. Cohen (London: Macmillan; New York: Oxford Univ. Press, 1979), I:77.
[4]The letter is in the Huntington Library, California.
[5]Sidney Herbert Williams and Falconer Madan, *A Handbook of the Literature of the Rev. C. L. Dodgson (Lewis Carroll)* (London: Humphrey Milford, 1931).
[6]*Huntington Library Bulletin,* 6 (November 1934), pp. 153-63; rpt. as Appendix IV to Ayres' *Carroll's Alice* (New York: Columbia Univ. Press, 1936).

fect, making the picture a more integral part of the story. Again, on p. 77 two lines are taken back to p. 76, so that the text directly below the picture of the Footmen relates directly to the picture ("The Fish-Footman began by producing from under his arm . . ."). Ayres briefly discussed the pictures, and conceded that in the 1866 edition they were "reproduced a little lighter, the effect being to make Alice rather prettier, her eyes and hair lighter, and her countenance brighter."

W. H. Bond went into the matter fully in an authoritative article.[7] He found that the book was set up from a foul case, and cited the two forms of the lower-case t as a key instant. He then discussed the so-called "dirtiness," which he concluded was due to "too much pressure and over-inking combining to produce a tendency to offset." He remarked "that the 'dirt' is offset, not from facing pages, but from the reverse side of the sheets involved, probably occurring when the sheets were stacked as they came off the press." I think this conclusion is incorrect.

The defect is not "offset" at all; it is due to "show-through," and is probably due to the use of a poor ink, containing too much vehicle for the pigment—the vehicle carries the pigment too far into the paper, so that it soaks in to the extent that it partially comes through the paper to show on the reverse side. It could not be offset from sheets stacked as they came off the press, as an examination of the pages shows that the "dirt" corresponds *exactly* with the type on the reverse side of the page. If offset, it might correspond closely but could not, except by the rarest of chances, do so exactly.

Bond was, however, very clear about the improvement in the reproduction of the illustrations. Use of the Hinman collating machine revealed that the blocks (with *one* exception, Bond said, but see below) were not redrawn or recut. The 1866 pictures were lighter, and the excess pressure and over-inking avoided. Bond showed clearly that Alice's face again and again is much improved. He discussed the alteration of one electrotype for the illustration on p. 29 where the top of the goose's head is ragged in the 1865 edition, but cut away leaving a gap in the 1866 edition. I don't know what copy of the 1866 he was using, but in fact the line is continuous in some copies (like mine), and is apparently the same as the 1932 china paper proofs, which suggests, contra-Bond, that a new electrotype *was* made. The other block to be altered, as Bond rightly described, was that of Alice with the long neck (p. 15).

Textually, Bond corrected Ayres' statement that Dodgson did not see proofs, and he noted 70 points of difference between the editions.

[7]"The Publication of *Alice's Adventures in Wonderland,*" *Harvard Library Bulletin,* 10 (1956), 306-24.

When I went through the texts, I found 89, or 78 if misprints and corrected misprints were excluded.[8]

Bond concluded that Dodgson was justified in his rejection of the 1865 *Alice,* and I would concur with his conclusion. His exposition of the improvement in the illustrations is compelling, but nevertheless I feel that the case is stronger for the rejection on account of the text rather than the illustrations. In spite of Bond's most relevant and persuasive case for the superiority of the 1866 over the 1865 illustrations, I still am not convinced that were it for *this reason alone,* the edition would have been rejected. It is difficult to escape from the fact that several highly respected Carroll scholars have found it difficult to come down wholly against the 1865 illustrations, from Williams in 1931 who found himself "at a loss to explain" the supposed defects, to Ayres who was lukewarm, and Warren Weaver (in his article on the Census—see below) who has looked at more copies of the 1865 printing than anyone else, and came down about equally "with an ambiguous score which favours sometimes the 1866 and sometimes the 1865." If I may include myself in such company, I found the differences between the illustrations in the rejected 60th Thousand of *Through the Looking-Glass* and the preceding 59th Thousand more marked than the differences between the 1865/1866 pictures in *Alice.*[9] Can we finally resolve the dilemma?

It is certainly true that the initial complaint came from Tenniel, who in his letter, quoted above, protested about the "disgraceful printing." It is significant that he does not specify the pictures. It was Dodgson who *quoted* Tenniel as being dissatisfied with the printing of the pictures. Is it not possible that Dodgson *assumed,* perhaps incorrectly, that Tenniel referred to the pictures simply because he was the artist? Commentators have pondered about the pictures, but all are unanimous in their condemnation of the printing—the two most important features being the foul case, and the show-through "dirt." The "dirt" coming through does affect the letterpress certainly, but is to an extent obscured by text on the other side of the leaf, which nearly coincide. But this of course is not so with the pictures, where time and again the clear areas are defaced by the show-through of type from the letterpress on the opposite side of the leaf. I suggest that it is this feature which Tenniel found so disgraceful. The fact that the printing of the pictures in 1866 is so much better is more due, I suggest, to the absence of this show-through. The findings by Bond of the

[8]See my "The Textual Alterations to *Alice's Adventures in Wonderland* 1865-1866," *Jabberwocky: Journal of the Lewis Carroll Society,* 3, No. 1 (Winter 1973), pp. 17-20.
[9]Selwyn H. Goodacre, "Lewis Carroll's Rejection of the 60th Thousand of *Through the Looking-Glass,*" *Book Collector,* 24, No. 2 (Summer 1975), pp. 251-256.

general improvement in the 1866 pictures may well be an unexpected bonus from the generally higher degree of skill in the printing, as a whole, by Clay. The fate of the rejected copies is well known. In April 1866, the sheets were bought by Appleton & Co. of New York. In May, "1000 Titles to Alice, American Edition" were printed by the Oxford University Press, and the cancel titles inserted after removal of the original title pages. As there were nearly 2000 copies, it was initially suggested that a second set of titles were printed in the USA, and two apparent variants seemed to support the theory. Bond, however, found that the Hinman machine showed that the two variants were closer to each other than either were to the 1865 titles. It seems virtually certain that the cancel page was set up in duplicate. It should be noted that the 1931 *Handbook* suggestion that the half title is also a cancel is incorrect. The error was repeated in the 1962 *Lewis Carroll Handbook,* and its 1970 reprint. The new edition (1979, revised by Denis Crutch) silently omits this point, only mentioning the new tipped-in title page.

It used to be suggested that the "first" of the two variants was bound in England, and the "second" bound in the USA. But since both are the one printing it is likely that the binding would have been in the one place. No one so far has adduced any evidence for where that place might have been. I am, however, able to offer concrete evidence that they *were* bound in England. David Schaefer owns a copy of the "Appleton Alice" which lacks the spine. Examination of the remnants of the paper liner reinforcing the backs of the sewn gatherings reveals a printed London address (Old Kent Road).

II

As the years went by after Dodgson's death in 1898, it was gradually recognised that only a certain number of copies of the 1865 *Alice* had survived; their significance and value began slowly to be recognised. The *Athenaeum* began to discuss the 1865/1866 problem in 1900. In the *Book Buyer* in 1920, Ernest North stated that fewer than 10 copies survived. Williams in his 1924 *Bibliography of Lewis Carroll* spoke of 9 copies, while in the 1931 *Handbook* Williams and Madan said that "about 15 can still be traced." The first attempt to make a definite list of known copies was for the Columbia University Exhibition in 1932, where no fewer than 9 copies were actually on exhibition; the catalogue noted a further 5 copies and reported one as lost, and two others as having "turned up in the last few years."

In 1963, to celebrate the purchase by Warren Weaver of the "India Alice" (see below), Weaver and Alfred Berol privately printed a booklet *The India Alice,* and included in it a census compiled by Weaver. He listed 16 copies, with a note of two more copies "probably not now in existence," and a mention of "a few so-called 'mixed' copies." Weaver republished the article, revised, in *The Private Library* January 1965, and again noted the 16 copies. By the time he came to write his magnificent, authoritative article, "The First Edition of *Alice's Adventures in Wonderland:* A Census,"[10] he had located 19 copies, with an addendum mentioning a newly discovered copy. In his masterly analysis, Weaver travelled the world to handle personally every copy, a feat that can probably never be repeated.

Since his article was published, I have been able to locate another three copies, two of which I have personally handled, and one for which I have the fullest of details. It seems a good time to revise and update the census.

In the Introduction to his census, Weaver offered some thoughts as to how many copies could possibly have survived. None of us can be certain, but it is useful to go over the ground again, and perhaps come to some further conclusions.

We know that 2000 sets of sheets were printed, and that Dodgson asked for 50 copies to be bound. We can group the various copies that are known. Firstly there is Carroll's own copy, bound in vellum, probably destined for Alice Liddell, but in the event not given; then there is the other vellum copy that he gave to Marion Terry, and which she returned to him, and which he kept all his life. There are three presentation copies (to Mrs. Lillie-Craik, Vere-Bayne, Christ Church), two copies owned by people known to Carroll (Rhoda Kitchen, Dalziel), and one copy given (?) by Carroll to a Printer's daughter (Alice Thomas). Thus far, eight.

We know from the Journal, that 34 copies were returned and were then distributed to a number of hospitals and children's homes, and to Dr. Southey and the Rev. W. Jacobson for them to give to needy children (for the sake of clarity I shall call all these "hospital" copies). Two definite hospital copies have survived (India Alice, Harewood). Thus far, ten. There are a theoretical 32 more hospital copies, which if added to the known 10 copies above makes 42, not a long way from the 50 copies bound at Dodgson's request. There seems no reason to doubt that any more than 50 were bound. When he called at Macmillan's to sign copies, it was only 19 days after the first copies had arrived; indeed, there may only have been the 20 or so copies there at

[10]*Papers of the Bibliographical Society of America,* 65, No. 1 (January-March 1971), pp. 1-40.

the time, as these were the only ones he signed—possibly the rest were to be sent to him when ready.

The remaining copies in the census would seem to have to be unrecognised hospital copies (but see below for two possible survivors of the printing shop). It is of interest that three copies have a piece cut out of the half title in just the place where Dodgson tended to write his inscriptions: one has a half title missing, one a front free end paper, and one a piece from the title page; these latter three defacements could well be due to removal of hospital ownership inscriptions. All these could be signed presentation copies that were returned, and then sent on to hospitals after removal of the inscription. There is a possibility that copies were sent for review, but it is difficult to see how any other copies could possibly exist. Weaver supposes that hospital copies could not long survive, but regulations in a Victorian children's home or hospital would be very different from today, and there may well have been rigid rules to be observed in the handling of books by the children. Curiously Weaver seems to imply that the 20 copies (or more) signed on 15 July are quite separate from the 34 returned copies, and makes a total of 54, by simple addition. This is quite fallacious, as I have outlined above—many of the hospital copies will have been returned presentation copies, or copies held by Carroll up to the rejection.

Alice was a book that became famous within a year of publication; copies would tend to be preserved once the quality began to be fully appreciated. Of the 23 copies in the census, 11 can be traced to their origin (the above 10 plus the proof copy), two more may possibly be survivors from the printer's shop, which leaves 10 which may be unrecognised hospital copies, which suggests that 22 copies have fallen by the wayside. In the tentative sum above, I suggested a total of 42 copies could be "explained," which leaves a further theoretical 8 copies. Whether a further 30 copies will ever turn up seems unlikely in the extreme, but the possibility is there!

In his census, Weaver boldly listed the copies in order of superiority. I have slightly amended the list, but have in general followed his guidelines, of giving precedence to inscribed copies, then original cloth, then rebound copies with original boards bound in. I have retained the unique proof copy at the head, but it now has no number, as it is not strictly an example of the published edition. I have included the lost Christ Church copy, on account of its great interest. Following Weaver's example, I initially give a straight list of all known copies, before discussing them individually. The figures and numbers in parentheses refer to the three earlier censuses—in order: Columbia Exhibition 1932; *India Alice* 1963; Weaver 1971 Census. "N" refers to a note only, the number in Copy No. 5 is a page reference. For the benefit of those without access to Weaver's article, I summarise the essential physical features of each copy.

Proof copy: Thomas—Alder-Barrett—Berol—Bobst   (— 1 1)

1. Carroll—Stuart—Williamson—Amory—Harvard   (N 3 5)
2. MAB—Carroll—Samuel—White—Rosenbach   (2b 2 2)
(3.) Dodgson—Christ Church   (N 17 N)
4. Lillie—Craik—Rosenbach—Johnson—Kettaneh—Wapner—
   Princeton   (2 5 4)
5. Vere—Bayne—Gribbel—Rosenbach—Rabinowitz—
   Berol—Bobst, "The Lost Alice"   (362 4 3)
6. Montague—Swathling—Rosenbach—Johnson—Kettaneh—
   Schiller   (2a 11 8)
7. Dalziel—Arthur—Huntington   (N 7 6)
8. Kitchin—Rosenbach—Pforzheimer—Borland—Self   (2d 8 9)
9. Coombe—St. Raphael—Harewood—(Bodleian)   (— — 11)
10. Metropolitan—Cousins—Kent—Morgan—Weaver—Texas
    "The India Alice"   (— 9 10)
11. Thomas—Harmsworth—Gloucester—British Library   (N 6 7)
12. Sharp—National Library of Scotland   (— — —)
13. Partridge—Davis   (— — N)
14. Lilly—Indiana   (— 10 15)
15. Amory—Harvard   (N 13 14)
16. Silver—Newberry   (— — 19)
17. Rogers—Yale   (2g 15 17)
18. Wells—Randall—Bodmer   (— 16 18)
19. Pease—Houghton   (2f 14 13)
20. Private ownership (London)   (— — —)
21. Edwards—Kern—Rosenbach—Young—New York Public
    Library   (2e 12 16)
22. Cross—Bath   (— — 12)

Weaver also mentions the presentation copy to Princess Beatrice, but see below (N 18 N); and the "mixed" copy at the Morgan Library (2c N N). In addition there are records of possibly 4 more copies. I discuss these at the close.

Proof Copy: Thomas—Alder-Barrett—Berol—Bobst (— 1 1)
    Plain red cloth (binding by a relative of John Thomas, who worked in the Oxford University Press in 1865), "somewhat shabby."
    Weaver deals very fully with the history of this fine copy. It may be

added that since Alfred Berol died in 1974, his entire collection has passed to the Elmer Holmes Bobst Library in New York University.

1. *Carroll—Stuart—Williamson—Amory—Harvard* (N 3 5)

Original white vellum presentation binding, dark green label on spine with title, binding decoration similar to standard red cloth binding.

Weaver curiously only places this great copy at No. 5, yet it is one of the two copies retained by Carroll all his life. The superb presentation binding is illustrated nearly full size on p. 76 of *The Houghton Library 1942-1967* (Cambridge, Mass.: Harvard College Library, 1967). It would appear that this copy was the one originally intended for Alice Liddell, but not given (since there is no inscription), in the event of the rejection.

2. *MAB—Carroll—Samuel—White—Rosenbach* (2b 2 2)

Rebound in white vellum, by Riviere in 1899.

This very fine copy is given second place, in spite of the rebind, on account of its illustrious history as one of the copies retained by Carroll till his death and because of the autograph MS poem. Weaver records the sale of the Stuart Samuel collection at the Southeby sale in 1907, in which this copy was item 31. His transcription is not too accurate. It in fact reads:

Carroll (Lewis) i.e. C.L. Dodgson. Alice's Adventures in Wonderland, FIRST EDITION, with 42 illustrations by John Tenniel, vellum extra, with elegant borders of flowers and leaves on the sides, the centres symbolically tooled, g.e. by Riviere; from "Lewis Carroll's" sale   8vo. Macmillan, 1865

On the fly-leaf is a poem of 12 lines in manuscript, by the author to M.A.B., inserted are five of the original drawings, and several proofs of the engravings. Only a few copies are known with the above date, and this copy is apparently on large paper.

Weaver ponders on the name of the original owner; is her name Marion (Terry) or Mary Anne Bessy, or Mary Anne Bessie? Morton Cohen in a note in *The Letters of Lewis Carroll* gives her baptismal name as Mary Anne Bessy, and adds "she later adopted the name Marion (for the stage) but was known affectionately as Polly." Denis Crutch has surmised that Bessie was spelt with "ie" to give the correct number of lines in the acrostic poem in the presentation copy of *The Snark* (see *Collected Verse of Lewis Carroll,* London: Macmillan, 1932, p. 236). Weaver notes the differences between the text of the dedicatory poem in this copy, and the copy of the 1866 edition of *Alice* (see below), but it should be noted that the second dash is line 8 not line 7 as stated by Weaver.

It would seem that this copy was given to MAB, and that it was returned as requested by Carroll, who later presented her with a copy of the 1866 *Alice* also bound for presentation in full dark blue morocco, with the same poem (slightly altered) as above. This 1866 copy is now in the National Library of Scotland; Hugh Sharp, the owner, was killed in a train crash in 1938, and his mother and sister presented his collection to the National Library in his memory.

(3.) *Dodgson—Christ Church* (N 17 N)

Original red cloth, fine condition.

This copy Weaver tells us disappeared from the library of Christ Church sometime between 1924 and 1928. It is described in the 1931 *Handbook,* where it is the copy from which Williams made the printed collation. He records, "I have . . . seen and examined what is probably the finest copy in existence of the 1865 Alice, and it was from this copy that the above collation was made. It contains the following inscription in Dodgson's handwriting. "Presented to the Common / Room, Ch. Ch. / by the Author / followed by the characteristic scrawled line." W. G. Hiscock, in a letter to *The Times Literary Supplement,* 7 May 1964, recorded that the book was on view on 2 June 1924, when the Oxford Bibliographical Society visited the Library to see a collection of Carrolliana. Williams made his collation on that day. When Hiscock catalogued the Carroll material at Christ Church soon after his appointment in 1928, the book could not be found. In March 1931, the former librarian W. H. Blunt recorded "it is shabby and no way remarkable looking copy." Hiscock doubted Blunt's view: "his sight had been failing for some time; and his statement can doubtless be disregarded." Morris Parrish, a stickler for condition, said his recollection of its condition "is that it was quite reverse" (i.e., of shabby). Williams confirmed his impression in 1936 and also observed that the inscription was "to the best of my belief and remembrance (I may say I am sure) on the half title."

From Williams' *Handbook* account, the copy would appear to be complete, though there is a mistake in the collation—the second signature [b] is not signed. Williams also says that there is one fine line over the text on p. 190, which if true is at variance with every other record of this feature, which is that there are two lines.

4. *Lillie—Craik—Rosenbach—Johnson—Kettaneh—Wapner— Princeton* (2 5 4)

Original red cloth, good condition, small water stain on back cover; inscribed presentation copy.

Weaver rightly suggests that this copy was presented for somewhat formal reasons rather than because Mrs. Craik was a close friend of Carroll's. This would seem incontrovertible, since he only met her for the first time a week before the copy was inscribed. It could well have been that Dodgson wished to present a copy to George Lillie Craik, who had handled Macmillan's negotiations, and that Craik suggested his wife as a more suitable recipient.

Weaver is misleading on the provenance. He says the book was recorded in the Sotheby sale on 3 April 1928 as coming from the library of Clement Shorter. This is wrong. Certainly part of the same sale *was* from the Clement Shorter collection, but this copy of the 1865 *Alice* (Lot No. 317) is recorded as the property of Mrs. Richards, of Blindwell, Nether Stowey, Somerset, and a note adds that she was the adopted daughter of the original recipient. The copy thus joins the elite as one with an uninterrupted provenance from its original presentation.

This copy, along with Kettaneh's other copy (No. 6), came on the market again on 20 May 1980 at a sale at the Hotel Drouot in Paris. The catalogue for the sale included a facsimile of the presentation inscription. The book was purchased by the well-known dealer, John Fleming. It then passed to Raymond W. Wapner, long-time treasurer of the Lewis Carroll Society of North America and partner in the book dealing firm of Justin G. Schiller, Ltd., of New York. Later in 1980 it was fully repaired and restored to fine condition by the conservator at the Pierpont Morgan Library; photographic documentation of the restoration was made, and the copy has now passed to the Princeton University Library, where it now forms part of the illustrious Morris Parrish collection, filling a gap which had long been a source of regret to all admirers of this great Lewis Carroll collection.

5. *Vere—Bayne—Gribbel—Rosenbach—Rabinowitz—Berol—Bobst "The Lost Alice"* (362 4 3)

Original red cloth, somewhat stained and chipped. Signed presentation copy to Carroll's old friend and Christ Church colleague.

The engaging story of this fine copy is nicely related by Weaver. As with the proof copy, this copy is now part of the Elmer Holmes Bobst Library of New York University.

6. *Montague—Swathling—Rosenbach—Johnson—Kettaneh—Schiller* (2a 11 8)

Bound in 1899, leaves untrimmed. Contains ten original drawings by Tenniel, with an autograph note by Tenniel on the half-title.

As described under Copy 4 (Lillie—Craik) this unique copy came on the market again, in 1980 at the Hotel Drouot in Paris. It was acquired by Justin G. Schiller, the well-known New York book dealer and Carroll scholar. He kindly arranged for me to examine the volume, so we can supplement Weaver's brief description. Weaver adds more or less as an afterthought that this is the "tallest and uncut copy." In fact this is a most significant statement. We know it was bound by Riviere in 1899 for L. S. Montague, with the leaves uncut. It is Mr. Schiller's contention that this means the sheets were unbound at the time (otherwise they would have been already trimmed), and therefore then the 1899 binding was the first time they were bound at all. This must be correct, and with the half title being signed by John Tenniel, it is tempting to suggest that the sheets belonged to him at one time. The unique features of the copy, it could be suggested, qualify it to be considered separately, in like manner to the proof copy (copy — 1 1).

Weaver mentions the "numerous notes and corrections by Carroll, all in purple ink." But it seems unlikely that they are in fact by Carroll; there appears to be no obvious (or unobvious) reason for the marks, which are difficult to interpret. None of them represent any correction or alteration that was realised in any later edition. The only suggestion that holds any credence is that they represent some type of marking of particular passages where the printing is not good. But this is mere conjecture.

The frontispiece/title page opening and p. 91 with the original Tenniel pencil drawing of the same picture (Alice and Cheshire-Cat) are illustrated in *Early Children's Books and Their Illustration* (New York: Pierpont Morgan Library, 1975).

7. *Dalziel—Arthur—Huntington* (N 7 6)
Original red cloth "essentially mint condition."

I was tempted to place this copy as No. 1 in view of its condition, but instead I have given precedence to inscribed copies. Weaver records that it was sold at a Sotheby auction to T. G. Arthur, and sold again as part of his estate in 1914 to the book dealer George Smith, who sold it to Huntington in 1916.

8. *Kitchin—Rosenbach—Pforzheimer—Borland—Self* (2d 8 9)
Original red cloth, slightly loose and worn.

Weaver persists in calling Xie Kitchin, Rhoda, but in every other reference to this close friend of Lewis Carroll's she is referred to by the diminutive form of her first name, Alexandra. Weaver states that Xie "received it from Carroll," but this hardly seems likely as she was only one year old in 1865, not an age of child that held much interest for Carroll. In any case, there is no presentation inscription, and it is inconceivable that Carroll would not have inscribed it if it were a gift. Her father, George William Kitchin, on the other hand was a colleague at Christ Church. More significantly he was Secretary of the School Book Committee for the University Press in October 1865, and in March 1866 Secretary to the Board of Delegates. He may well have picked up a copy in the course of his duties. He then could have passed the copy onto his daughter, when she was of an age to appreciate it. Since the Weaver census, the Pforzheimer Library sold the copy to Ms. Harriet Borland through the Chicago book dealers Hammil and Barker. Ms. Borland's bookplate is now on the inside front cover. William Self acquired the copy from Ms. Borland, via the same dealers "several years ago" (personal letter to the writer from Mr. Self).

9. *Coombe—St. Raphael—Harewood—(Bodleian)* (— — 11)
Original red cloth, slightly frayed, front cover bent.

This is the first of the two proven "hospital copies." Denis Crutch has surmised that M. Coombe could be a misreading of "Mr. W. Combe," the printer to the University, who figures several times in Carroll's diaries, concerning the printing of the 1865 *Alice.* What more natural thing than for the printer to take a copy for himself? As with several copies (13 and 14), a small piece has been removed from the half-title. Could this missing piece have carried the original presentation signature, removed when returned, and prior to it being given away? One could surmise that it was later re-acquired by Coombe, who made a note of his original receipt of it from Carroll. It may be significant that the new note (not in Dodgson's hand) reads, "Given to M. Coombe by its Author The Rev. C. L. Dodgson." Coombe, of course, would have known of the author's identity. The copy is at present owned by "a senior member of Oxford University, who wishes to remain anonymous but states that it will ultimately be presented or left by him to the Bodleian Library."

10. *Metropolitan—Cousins—Kent—Morgan—Weaver—Texas*
"The India Alice" (— 9 10)
Original red cloth, rubbed and with small stains, most of the front free end paper missing.

Weaver recounts the romantic story of this copy in his census. It is the second of the proven "hospital copies," and was discovered by L. C. Kent-Morgan on the floor of a bookshop in Bangalore, India, where he bought it for Re.1/8, i.e., 2/3d. It was sold at Hodgson's rooms on 14 December 1961, lot 242. An anecdotal account of the sale is given by O. F. Snelling in *The Antiquarian Book Monthly Review* (February 1982). Certain details were corrected in the April 1982 issue by Justin G. Schiller and the present writer. The title page of this volume is one of the illustrations in Weaver's own account of his collection in *The Library Chronicle of the University of Texas* (November 1970). It was no doubt the stimulus of the acquisition of this lovely copy that led him into compiling his census.

11. *Thomas—Harmsworth—Gloucester—British Library* (N 6 7)

Original red cloth, somewhat worn and soiled, "the binding of the spine of the book has been tightened" (British Library report).

The story of this fine copy is fully told by Weaver; it was given by Frank Thomas to his daughter, Alice, following the example of his brother John (see above—proof copy). Weaver suggests that the volume was originally bound by the same member of the Thomas family who bound the proof copy—in spite of the Sotheby auction note that the book was "in the original red cloth binding, but had at one time been skillfully recased (apparently by an amateur binder)." Weaver has been misled. In fact the volume is a regular first edition, in the original genuine cloth boards—the Burn binders ticket is present on the end paste-down endpaper, and although Weaver says the lettering at the foot of the spine is illegible, when I examined the copy it was quite possible to make out the remains of MACMILLAN. There seems no reason to doubt the account given by Alder-Barrett (a descendant): "Lewis Carroll, whose permission he asked (to take a set of proofs to have them bound), had offered to give her a copy of the book instead. He did so and wrote her name in it." Possibly he was the more ready to do so in view of the little girl's name. Weaver says that the note (not in Carroll's writing) "Alice Fannie Thomas from the Author, 1867" is on the verso of the half-title; in fact, it is on the reverse of the front free endpaper. The letter to Tom Taylor from Carroll about possible titles for the book (pasted on the front endpaper) is reproduced in facsimile in the Sotheby catalogue for 26 March 1947 (the sale of the Harmsworth collection). Maggs bought the copy for £1,200. Weaver records that Maggs sold it to the Duke of Gloucester in 1952, but it seems more likely that Maggs was acting for the Duke in 1947, and that he returned it to Maggs in 1952 who sold it on his behalf to the British Museum in February of that year for £1320 (i.e., the original price plus 10% commission).

A curious feature of the pages is that the free edge of the leaves are slightly rounded off at the corners, especially at the base. Weaver measures the leaves as 5.2" x 7.7". I found them to be 5.1" x 7.5".

12. *Sharp—National Library of Scotland* (— — —)

Original red cloth, slightly scuffed.

John Hayward, in giving an account of the acquisition of the Alice Thomas copy by the British Museum (in *The Book Collector,* Summer 1952), mentioned that the only other copy recorded in the United Kingdom was the Hugh Sharp copy in the National Library of Scotland. Weaver missed the note, and never learned of the copy's existence. I have a full description, kindly supplied to me by John Morris, the assistant keeper.

The copy is in the original red cloth boards, with slight scuffing on both covers, and two ink stains on the upper. The cloth at the joints is frayed, badly along the upper board, and in one or two places on the lower. The corners are bumped and the head and foot of the backstrip are a bit tired. The roundels on the covers are rubbed. The lettering on the spine is legible, though the CO. of the lettering at the foot is lost. The typography on [b]^1 and [b]^2 indicates that the copy is variant A (Weaver explains that Variant A has "Alice! A . ." in the last verse of the dedicatory poem, and RABBIT HOLE in the list of contents; Variant B has "Alice! a . ." and RABBIT-HOLE). There is slight grubbiness on the title page and on p. 14 and p. 15, but otherwise the copy is good internally. The end papers are the original dark green, and the Burn label is present at the lower left hand corner of the back paste down end paper. The front free endpaper has been torn out. There is no indication of the provenance.

13. *Partridge—Davis* (— — N)

Original red cloth, signs of cleaning.

In the closing paragraph of his census, Warren Weaver referred to a copy of *Alice* in the original red cloth, "with a '65 title page and with points in each signature which assure that they are either Macmillan '65 or Appleton '66." He studied it carefully and sent it back to "the London dealer." The "London dealer" was Mr. David Batterham, the antiquarian bookseller; he was then acting for the executors of Mr. Robert Partridge, a former librarian, and a collector and dealer, who died in 1968. The book then appeared as Lot 311 in the sale of Children's Books etc. at Sotheby's on 19-20 April 1971. The catalogue description is subdued: "outer edge of title, frontispiece and protective tissue slightly frayed, reinserted, title soiled and worn, blank portion of half-title bearing ownership or presentation inscription removed, original cloth gilt, badly worn, repaired at top and bottom of spine." Some viewers of the volume appear to have thought the book might be a faked up copy, which may have accounted for the fact that it fetched "only" £950 to David Drummond, the West End dealer, bidding on behalf of John Davis, the well-known Carroll collector, and later Chairman of the Lewis Carroll Society. John Davis died in 1981, but his family have kindly allowed me to examine the copy. The binding is original, though showing signs of being cleaned; the edges are plain. The typography on [b]^1 and [b]^2 indicates that it is variant A. The original dark green end papers are present as is the Burn label. On the front paste down end paper is a little bookseller's ticket—"sold by Slatter & Rice, Oxford." The portion of the half-title that has been irregularly cut out measures about 3" x 1¾". A careful examination reveals that the title page and frontispiece are conjugate, although both stand a little proud of the rest of the book when closed, but the edges of the two leaves match exactly. There is a reinforcing strip on the reverse of the frontispiece. The pages measure 7 15/32" x 5 4/32". The title page is rather grubby, but otherwise the book is excellent internally.

In my opinion, the book is a genuine copy of the 1865 *Alice,* but it would have been reassuring to know more of its provenance. As Weaver pointed out, it would be enormously difficult to fake up a copy—one would need an Appleton Alice, and a conjugate frontispiece/title page of the 1865 *Alice;* the latter would be almost impossible to forge convincingly. The removal of the section of the half title closely corresponds with other copies (9, 14), another possible pointer to genuineness. Indeed, the presence of a bookdealer's Victorian label suggests that this could even be a copy that was on sale—locally in Oxford.

14. *Lilly—Indiana* (— 10 15)
Original red cloth, somewhat stained, recased.

There is little to add to Weaver's account, except to note that it is one of the copies with a section cut away from the half-title, possibly to remove a dedication (cf. copies 9, 13).

15. *Amory—Harvard* (N 13 14)
Rebound in full red polished morocco, original boards bound in at end.

16. *Silver—Newberry* (— — 19)
Rebound in full dark blue levant morocco by Riviere, original boards bound in at the end, cleaned and restored. Contains 5 original Tenniel drawings.

Weaver had reservations about the preliminaries, but the rebinding was too tight for full examination.

17. *Rogers—Yale* (2g 15 17)
Rebound in full levant red morocco by Zaehnsdorf, half-title missing, original boards bound in at the end.

Weaver tells us that this is the only copy known with the half-title missing. He wonders if it may be the same as the copy sold at Knight, Frank & Rutley on 7 February 1936, which was described as "original cloth (frayed), 1st blank wanting, few pages slightly torn." *The Times*

Literary Supplement for 15 February 1936 called that copy "a misery, childish scribbles here and there, binding faded and spine loose, front endpaper and first leaf torn out." In fact, it could not possibly be this Rogers copy, since this copy was reported as already rebound in 1932 when exhibited at the Columbia exhibition (see *India Alice,* p. 15); and in any case, it is difficult not to see "childish scribbles."

18. *Wells—Randall—Bodmer* (— 16 18)

Rebound in full polished red morocco, original back cover and spine bound in at the end.

19. *Pease—Houghton* (2f 14 13)

Rebound in full tooled crimson morocco by T. J. Cobden-Sanderson in 1898.

Weaver mentions that this copy included a letter from Alice Liddell dated 5 February 1833; this should read 5 February 1863. The letter is published in facsimile in Anne Clark's *The Real Alice* (London: Michael Joseph, 1981, pp. 76-77). There is also a letter to Mary Brown from Carroll, dated 1 January 1872 (this is not included in *The Letters of Lewis Carroll*). This fine copy is now on deposit at the Pierpont Morgan Library in New York, along with the rest of Houghton's collection. It featured at the Library's 1982 exhibition for the 150th anniversary of Lewis Carroll's birth.

20. *Private Ownership (London)* (— — —)

Rebound in full red morocco.

On BBC tv in February 1982, as part of a programme with the title "The Genuine Article," H. Bayntun-Coward of the well-known firm of book binders "George Bayntun" demonstrated how his firm had rebound a copy of the 1865 *Alice* for a private client in South London. After some private correspondence the owner allowed me to see this hitherto undeclared copy. The owner told me he had found the copy quite by chance in one of 9 or 10 bags of old books that had been left at his place of business. The copy was in poor condition, roughly bound in green cloth with no lettering on the spine or cover. He was advised to send it to Warren Weaver, who, late in 1971, made a thorough examination and a written report. The leaves measure 7 7/32" x 4 31/32", and the typography on [b]^1 and [b]^2 indicates variant A. There are some dirt marks on pp. 3, 32, 74 and 99, and small stains on pp. 108 and 109; pp. 134 and 135 are slightly dirty; there is a small injury to the paper on p. 163, and a small tear on p. 167; there is a small piece missing from the right hand margin of p. 179, and a small tear in the margin of pp. 182 and 192. The back end paper has a small piece missing from the margin. There is no evidence of cleaning or tampering. All the signatures are right for 1865. The end papers appear original but are white and foxed.

Weaver advised that it should be elegantly rebound, in view of the poor state, and the fact that the boards were not apparently original. George Bayntun accordingly took the book very carefully apart, into the original signature, full photographic records being taken throughout. [a]^2 and [a]^3 were found to be conjugate. The signatures had been stabbed through in five places, and roughly sewn together with thread. Bayntun rebound the volume most elegantly in full red morocco, with a single gold line round the front cover, and the White Rabbit with watch in the centre in gilt; the back cover has the gold line only. The title ALICE IN WONDERLAND is on the spine, with author, designs of cards, and the White Rabbit again, with the 1865 date at the base. All edges have been gilded, and the leaves now measure 7 3/32" x 4 25/32".

The paper of this unusual copy appears to be rather coarser than other copies I have seen, which makes one wonder if this is another example of a printer's reject rescued from the printer's shop—and who knows, by the third of the Thomas brothers?

21. Edwards—Kern—Rosenbach—Young—New York Public Library (2e 12 16)

Rebound in dark blue morocco.

It is interesting to note that this copy has a piece cut out from the title page (cf. copies 9, 12, 13, 14, 17).

22. Cross—Bath (— — 12)

Recased in a regular publication binding of the turn of the century.

Fully discussed by Weaver in his census. This copy was a chief exhibit in the exhibition organized by the Lewis Carroll Society in 1973 at Longleat House, the home of the Marquess of Bath, the owner of this copy.

This concludes all the copies of the true 1865 *Alice* that are known to exist, plus one that is lost. Weaver mentions another "lost" copy—the copy owned by the Duchess of Albany (N 18 N). In *The India Alice,* Weaver said, "This copy was exhibited at the Centennial Celebration at Columbia University." But this is not so. The Catalogue merely records that there is "one in the collection of the late Duchess of Albany." The only evidence that such a copy ever existed is in Collingwood's *The Life and Letters of Lewis Carroll* (London: T. Fisher Unwin, 1898, p. 104): "Miss Alice Liddell received the first presentation copy of Alice's Adventures in Wonderland; the second was sent to Princess Beatrice." That she had a copy of the 1866 *Alice* is undeniable—it was sold at Sotheby's on 16 March 1937, lot 295, where it is described as "in the original presentation binding of white vellum gilt." The note to the sale quotes the above passage and goes on: "That would be a copy of the 1865 edition; as is well known all recipients and purchasers of the 1865 edition were asked to return their copies, the 1866 edition being supplied in replacement. The copy now offered for sale is that replacement." Nicely brought up royal children would surely return a defective copy if requested by the author; it is, after all, only good manners. Weaver wrote to the daughter of the Duchess, Princess Alice, whose secretary replied, "She has no recollection of her mother's edition of *Alice in Wonderland,* but thinks it may have been given to her brother the Duke of Coburg, whose library was destroyed during the war." That is only conjecture by an old lady, and she did not mention the undoubted sale of the replacement 1866 *Alice.*

Weaver mentions one "mixed" copy—at the Pierpont Morgan Library (2c N N). It has sections from both editions; but is still of interest, as it is the copy used for the collation in the Williams 1924 *Bibliography.* (No wonder that that reads so oddly.)

Finally Weaver includes mention of copies that have figured in auction sales, but which do not appear to fit any copies in the census.

a. *T. G. Arthur* is said to have bought a copy in 1908 at a Sotheby sale. That he bought the Dalziel copy in 1889 seems undoubted, and this was sold as part of his library on 11 July 1914. The fate of the 1908 copy is nowhere recorded.

b. *Henry Clapp Smith—Gabriel Wells.* A "very poor copy," bought by Gabriel Wells in 1928.

c. *Gabriel Wells.* "tears, soiled, frayed, half morocco worn." Bought by Wells at a sale at Sotheby's on 15 April 1930.

d. *Maggs.* Bought by the London Antiquarian book dealers at a Knight, Frank & Rutley sale on 7 February 1930 (see above, in account of copy 17). I wrote to Maggs, to ask if they have any record of this purchase, but they did not have the sale catalogue which "would have told whether we bought it for stock or on commission."

One should add, perhaps, that (a), (b), and (d) *could* be earlier references to copies Nos. 3, 13, and 20.

The search goes on. Somewhere there is the lost Christ Church *Alice;* somewhere there may be three or four copies sold at auction that have gone to ground. Long may the search continue; it is all part of the enduring fascination of that greatest of children's books, *Alice's Adventures in Wonderland,* by Lewis Carroll, Macmillan 1865.

I am most grateful to those owners of copies who have been more than helpful in supplying me with details of their property: Justin G. Schiller, William Self, John Morris (of the National Library of Scotland), Edward Wakeling, The British Library, and June Davis; to Denis Crutch, who has lent a guiding hand throughout, and to the members of the Lewis Carroll Society (England) who joined a symposium on the 1865 *Alice* in October 1980; and to Edward Guiliano who encouraged me to finalise my thoughts for this paper. And finally to the memory of that great collector and enthusiast, the late Warren Weaver, who first stimulated us all in the search.

LEWIS CARROLL IN A CHANGING WORLD:
AN INTERVIEW WITH MORTON N. COHEN

Edward Guiliano

EG. We're here on the occasion of the 150th anniversary of Lewis Carroll's birth, but it's something of an anniversary for you too; you've been editing Carroll's letters for twenty years. Have there been significant changes in the public's and/or in academicians' perception and reception of Carroll since you took up the man in 1962?

MC. Well, Carroll seems to have a constant appeal to both specialized and general readers. Time doesn't take its toll on Carroll. If anything, we find new appropriations, new meanings, new applications of what he is, or what he was, what he stands for, and what his works are and what they stand for. At the Morgan Library exhibition the final tally of people who came to see the sesquicentennial exhibition was over 50,000, and the Morgan Library puts on some remarkable shows during a year: their usual annual total is about 100,000 people. For Carroll to bring in over 50,000 people in three months is really quite a record, isn't it?

EG. Would that have happened twenty years ago?

MC. I don't think so. There was certainly a lull in interest in Lewis Carroll between the 100th anniversary and the 150th anniversary. After the 100th anniversary in 1932 Carroll seemed to go into an eclipse, but after the Second World War there was a reawakening of interest which continues to gain momentum all the time. The new works that have come out, particularly the diaries in the early fifties, generated a great deal of interest. The psychological studies of Victorian writers also generated interest. It is astonishing to see all the children responding to Carroll today. You would think that they would find so Victorian a man, such archly Victorian works difficult to understand.

EG. An obvious explanation is that they are not understanding the man or the Victorian work; they are understanding Carroll our contemporary, to borrow that voguish phrase.

MC. That's the great virtue of Carroll. I don't think Carroll will ever die because his writing transcends nationality and time.

EG. Speaking of nationality and cultural perspective, from your experience—I know your work has taken you to England many times, and you have long maintained a home there—do you notice a dif-

ference between the way Americans and the British perceive and respond to Carroll?

MC. Not really. One of the worst things I ever heard was the President of the Lewis Carroll Society at one of their meetings in London actually wonder aloud whether any Americans truly understand the *Alice* books. The implied doubt is absurd. Some Americans understand the *Alice* books better than many English people simply because they have read so much. After all, we are steeped in English culture, and we share the literary tradition.

EG. Is the experience of the two peoples with the Alice *books the same, though?*

MC. I think they largely are the same. The important thing about the *Alice* books is not the treacle well or the rabbit hole but Alice herself and childhood transcendent, childhood in general, not Victorian childhood. What's important is Lewis Carroll's ability to get into the child's mind and see through the child's eyes the utter confusion of adult society. He confronts the dilemma of every child: "How do I adjust to this mad world?" This is what any child, no matter where, will feel when he reads the *Alice* books. Whether he or she is consciously aware of it or not, the child realizes that this kid Alice had a rough time of it just like I'm having, but she made it, and I'm going to make it too.

EG. How did Carroll make it in his own day? How was he regarded in his lifetime by the Oxford community, and how is he regarded there today?

MC. The Oxford community of Carroll's time was a stern, upper-crust, churchy, academic community. They accepted Carroll well enough. Certainly they respected him for his accomplishments. Lion hunters, when they learned that he was Lewis Carroll and not just Charles Dodgson the mathematician, went after him hammer and tongs; they loved to have him for dinner parties and show him off. And many mothers advanced friendships with their daughters because they felt that they were touching greatness. Some people, of course, objected to Lewis Carroll having little girls to tea in his rooms at Christ Church; or if they didn't object, they snickered and gossiped about it, but as Carroll himself says, if you only do things that people approve of, you'll do nothing in your life. It didn't faze him. He lived the life that he wanted to live; he lived his life fully, and he lived it hard. He lived it many hours a day. He did the things he thought were right to do and the things he enjoyed doing. He got on fine, and the Oxford society managed to accommodate him. Today, Carroll is far less important; Oxford is much bigger, less of a social community than it was then. My experience at Christ Church was rather interesting. In the early days I thought that Carroll would be considered one of the great historical presences at Christ Church. But I detected a very distinct resentment to Carroll, particularly because every time one went out into Tom Quad one ran into a group of tourists flashing cameras and asking where Lewis Carroll had lived. Of course, the dons of Christ Church wondering about a diminished ninth or puzzling over commentaries on certain parts of the Old Testament are not going to warm at being stopped by seekers for Lewis Carroll's rooms. They thought, and perhaps still think, that Christ Church should be known better for all the Prime Ministers, the royalty, the aristocracy, the Indian Viceroys who got their degrees or were resident at The House rather than for Lewis Carroll. But after a while I found that the dons, some of them anyway, accepted me as part of the Christ Church community, and were interested in Lewis Carroll, at least up to a point.

EG. Let's go back again to Victorian Oxford for a few moments, and let me ask you some questions about the man. I know you used to dismiss Caryl Hargreaves' claim that Dodgson wanted to marry his mother, Alice Liddell. You've recently changed your mind. Why?

MC. Actually, I didn't change my mind recently; I changed it in 1969 when I first got a photocopy of the diaries from the family. When I sat down and read through the diaries, the complete diaries not just the published excerpts—somewhere between 25 and 40% was never published, and naturally those unpublished bits and pieces are enormously significant. Those were the parts that the family decided should not be published. Roger Lancelyn Green, who edited the diaries, actually never even saw the full unpublished diaries because he worked from an edited typescript. When I first read through the unpublished portions of the diaries, however, I realized that another dimension to Lewis Carroll's "romanticism" existed. Of course it is pretty hard to reconcile the stern, Victorian clergyman with the man who favored little girls to a point where he would want to propose marriage to one or more of them. I believe now that he made some sort of proposal of marriage to the Liddells, not saying "may I marry your eleven-year-old daughter," or anything like that, but perhaps advancing some meek suggestion that after six or eight years, if we feel the same way that we feel now, might some kind of alliance be possible? I believe also that he went on later on to think of the possibility of marrying other girls, and I think that he would have married. He was a marrying man. I very firmly believe that he would have been happier married than as a bachelor, and I think one of the tragedies of his life was that he never managed to marry.

EG. That's an important revelation.

MC. It is a major revelation.

EG. And it is just the sort of fuel psychoanalytic critics have been looking for to reread all of Carroll's imaginative works in terms of sexual repression or unfulfilled desires.

MC. Yes, he was repressed but he was a "successfully repressed" man. He had all the usual sexual impulses: he wrote about marriage; he said that God gave us sexual desires, but he added that they had to be fulfilled only in marriage both for reproduction and for the pleasure in reproduction. He would have loved to have had his own children, and he would have been a wonderful father. Married, he would have been provoked to much higher and better flights of fancy than as a bachelor. I base my entire change of mind and my new approach to this particular aspect of Carroll on historical record. I am not interested in psychoanalyzing him, and I am not really interested in wild speculation.

EG. But you are at least saying that there was, and I guess I must use the word, an erotic element in his life and at least a covert sexual attraction between Carroll and these young girls.

MC. I think in some cases, yes. I think there was an equally strong aesthetic attraction. It is difficult, perhaps impossible, to draw the line between sexual attraction and aesthetic attraction.

EG. That's the problem we have with his photographs, it seems to me. The nude photographs can be troubling. Certainly the four that you brought to light are artistically ambitious, creative, and unusual; but I have a hard time reconciling them with the more blatantly "suggestive" ones—Alice as beggar child, the various bare-foot child-friends in night gowns or lying on couches, and also the photograph, if it's genuine, of Maud Constance Meulbury that Graham Ovenden attributes to Carroll and publishes in Victorian Children.

MC. That photograph is not by Carroll. I'm sorry; I reject that entirely. That's not a Carroll photograph. It couldn't possibly be. I would not allow it in that group. But considering the photographs you mentioned earlier, the ones in the Rosenbach Foundation, the beggar child, and the others, I find them perfectly acceptable from the standpoint of the history of art photography. I think of course that both beauty and sexual attraction are in the eyes of the beholder. If one finds those photographs pornographic, that's one's own assessment and not necessarily a reflection on Lewis Carroll.

EG. So it is a kind of libidinous twentieth-century hindsight.

MC. We're dealing with an age of very primitive art photography, don't forget, and we're also dealing with an age where sexless girls as butterflies, and fairies in gardens, and illustrations of sexless children in all kinds of books were very acceptable. He wouldn't have anything to do with boys because you can't conceal a boy's sex, you see. He liked boys. The charge that he hated boys is false. He is his own worst enemy on that point, though, because he makes a joke of it all the time, and people quote him seriously, the way they do Hamlet saying "What a rogue and peasant slave am I." But those photographs are perfectly acceptable in the history of photography and the history of the Victorian notion of what a little girl looks like undressed.

EG. You dismiss as myth the notion that Carroll disliked boys. How about the notion that Carroll broke off relations with young girls when they reached puberty?

MC. He never did break off the relationships; they broke them off. He held on to as many relationships as he could. He loved it when they became, as he says in so many of his letters, a woman-friend after they had been a "child-friend." And he welcomed their husbands, their fiancés; and, when they had children of their own, he took up with the children and gave them presents and took them to theaters. He loved that sort of thing. His great lament, over and over again, is how many child-friends leave where "the stream and river meet." *They* break off with him, not *he* with them.

EG. Let's turn to the letters. And the very first question to begin with is, how did you become interested in Lewis Carroll and editing his letters? Why Lewis Carroll?

MC. Well, I am a Victorian specialist as you know, and, before the Lewis Carroll letters, I edited a smaller volume of letters from Rudyard Kipling to Rider Haggard. And my oldest friend in England is Roger Lancelyn Green, whom I first met in 1954. As you know, he edited the diaries, through the Dodgson family, and he actually suggested that he and I edit the letters. I wasn't able to do it when he suggested it since I was already in the middle of another book. We later talked about it again, and it happened. Then Roger got very much involved in other things, and rather left it to me to carry forward.

EG. You certainly didn't anticipate a twenty-year . . .

MC. No, and I'm glad I didn't because I never would have started had I anticipated such a long trial. But of course I could have done it much more quickly. I didn't have to stand in line at Somerset House and St. Catherine's House checking all those registers for the births, deaths, marriages, wills, of these little girls. But I knew that if I didn't pluck those girls from history, then no one ever would. So, here was the chance really for us to get to see who the girls were that Dodgson was interested in. I recognize that I stood at a rather critical time in the history of this kind of work, when the Victorians were still available for another few moments. When I first started getting birth certificates at Somerset House, I paid six pence, six old pennies [about 7¢] for a birth certificate, you now pay one pound, seventy-five pence [about $3.15]. How many of those certificates could an editor afford today? And there are other problems of that sort.

EG. Every time someone mentions Carroll as a letter writer, they quote the magical number of 98,721 that appeared in his letter register. We know, though, that it was a register of letters received and sent. How many letters do you think Carroll wrote? And also, how many letters were you able to trace?

MC. In my files I have copies of over four thousand letters by Carroll, and letters still keep pouring in. I'm still keeping a complete file in the hope that someday a supplement to the basic two volumes may appear, not necessarily edited by me, but I intend to make all of this material publicly available at some central depository. In a letter to the editor of *Jabberwocky,* the journal of the Lewis Carroll Society in England, I concluded that Carroll wrote no fewer than 100,000 letters. I went through various mathematical gyrations to prove that.

EG. So we can bandy about that 100,000 figure with impunity?

MC. Yes, I think we're quite safe in saying Carroll himself wrote at least 100,000 letters in his lifetime. Do you know there was a second letter register, one that has not survived, a register that he kept as Curator of Christ Church Senior Common Room where he entered all the letters he wrote and received in the nine-and-a-half years he served in that post. And I don't believe anyway he recorded every little letter he wrote.

EG. He didn't record every little event in his life in his journals. You began searching for Carroll's letters in 1962, that's a time when you were still able to go directly to people who knew Carroll, including some of his child-friends.

MC. Yes, I met a good many charming old ladies in my search for Carroll letters. It was a great pleasure. I suppose the connection with whom I had the closest relationship was his actual niece, Irene Dodgson Jaques. Well, I attended her last birthday party, ninety-sixth, a couple of years ago. We got on wonderfully. I'd go home and at night try to type up the essence of our little conversations—she knew that too, she kept telling me stories. We loved sitting around talking about "Uncle Charles," as we called him. She called me "Cousin Morton" by then. She was thirteen when Carroll died, you see, so she knew him almost as an adult and remembered him vividly.

EG. There must have been moments of great discovery along the way, but, on the other hand, moments of despair or frustration. In order for you to come up with 4,000 letters lots of people had to be very generous, and you had to have had access to public and private collections. What were some of the problems you faced?

MC. Some people are not so generous about these things. They live with the old notion that if letters are published their commercial value diminishes, which isn't at all true any more. I've sat in the auction halls tabulating the differences in prices that the published letters bring and the unpublished letters bring, and there isn't a real distinction. But people cannot easily be convinced about this. I know for a fact that a good number of collectors withheld their collections from me, didn't even surface, for fear that I might publish the letters they had and which they considered great commercial investments. Most large collectors and most large libraries, of course, gave me copies of all their holdings freely. I had trouble with one private collector who wanted to buy the diaries from the Dodgson family and who insisted, as a price for sharing his letters, that I intercede to get the family to sell him the diaries, and I just wouldn't do that. He consequently did not allow me in his lifetime to have access to his letters; but he died and his family gave his whole collection to a major university, and then I instantly had access to all those letters. That episode rather delayed publication by a year because I was all ready to go to press before those letters became available. At this point, there are no major Lewis Carroll holdings that have not been made available.

EG. The large two-volume edition came out in 1979, and you mention in your Preface that you have collected many more letters. Certainly the edition is weighted in favor of letters to the child-friends and is designed overall for a reasonably broad audience. What about some of the other letters, the more specialized ones, the ones you suggested would be forthcoming in new volumes. What can we anticipate seeing soon?

MC. I wouldn't call the basic two-volume edition a *selection* at all. Given my files and the collection of letters now available, we already have *collected* letters of Lewis Carroll. The things that I left out are four specialized sets of letters, which are forthcoming. I'll talk about them in a minute. But setting those four specialized sets of letters aside, those left out are really superfluous and esoteric letters that would do no one any good. Many are unintelligible because they are on matters mathematical or theological, and when their opposite numbers are missing they become meaningless. All the good letters, all the meaningful letters available to me, all the letters that throw any kind of light—biographical, historical—have been included in the two volumes. That is, all that were available to me. I did omit four sets of letters intentionally, but even they are not all omitted; in each case I have included a dozen or so representative examples of the specialized letters. One set is the letters that passed between Lewis Carroll and the House of Macmillan. The second is the letters that passed between Lewis Carroll and his illustrators. Third are all the public letters, letters that Lewis Carroll sent to the press and reproduced either in print or by means of some other method such as his electric pen; these are what we call "circular" letters, those reproduced and sent to more than one person.

EG. How many of them are there?

MC. Hundreds really, all together. And the fourth set is all the letters about producing *Alice* on the stage; there are some ninety letters to Henry Savile Clarke, there is the play text, reviews of the play, music for the play, and a lot of peripheral material that goes with that. Those four sets will appear as separate volumes. Two are being worked on at the moment.

EG. Which two?

MC. The House of Macmillan letters and the Savile Clarke letters. Anita Gandolfo, a former student and research assistant of mine, is co-editing the House of Macmillan letters with me. Regina Domeraski, also a former research assistant and Ph.D. student of mine at the CUNY Graduate Center, is co-editing the Savile Clarke. We're working on those two volumes rather well. Cambridge University Press has agreed to publish the House of Macmillan set as part of a series of books on Victorian publishing. But it's a hard job. There is a lot of work in those letters. We're not going to be able to publish them completely. Two thousand letters survive: a thousand Lewis Carroll letters, a thousand Macmillan letters. Cambridge is allowing us to print about six hundred. You see it's not our choice at all; publishing costs and limitations cramp our work. That volume will take another couple of years before it goes to press because so much work needs to be done.

EG. That means 1984-ish at best.

MC. I think so. The Savile Clarke volume could be done sooner. We might even hope for that to go to press in '83, December 1983. It is well along, all transcribed, largely annotated; I did a lot of the annotations originally, you see, because I thought they were all going to go into the big massive edition.

EG. I'm sure if you gave Carrollians the choice of which of the four volumes they would want first, it would be the volume on the illustrators.

MC. I know, but that will be the hardest of the lot. And I have not found anywhere the co-editor whom I want to have, someone who knows a great deal about nineteenth-century book production and illustration.

EG. I think you are announcing your need here.

MC. Yes. I myself am not as qualified to deal with the art material as I should like to be.

EG. What are the responsibilities of an editor of collected letters?

MC. An editor of collected letters must produce a perfectly readable, beautiful book. This is so important but seemingly hard to achieve. Ovid said that art is to conceal art, and, in that spirit, an editor must be absolutely nobody; he must live in the shadows of the work, and never step forward truly as a personality there.

EG. It is very hard though when you are editing letters, when you are selecting letters, not to step forward. You said a minute ago that there were some incomprehensible letters on mathematics.

MC. Yes, one makes decisions quietly all the time. I made many quiet decisions correcting Lewis Carroll's errors that the reader would not know about. But I am working quietly and not showing my face. It is the editor's first responsibility to present the text as readable as possible and to let Lewis Carroll, or any subject, emerge in the most facile, unencumbered way possible and to add unobtrusively the information that is necessary to portray Lewis Carroll accurately. That's what the editor's job is. Editors sometimes forget that; they are more concerned with reproducing the writing with all its quirks and oddities, even if the quirks and oddities are of no use and don't help us to understand the writer. They obstruct the reader, for instance, by printing all kinds of wild, irrelevant, unmeaningful punctuations.

EG. Again that is an editorial judgment. One would hardly censor the punctuation of Emily Dickinson or Shaw, and yet one can hear an editor saying, well this is idiosyncratic, let's make it more readable.

MC. Nevertheless, the text must, above all, be readable. If one doesn't make it readable, one fails as an editor. Just as I am devoted to an unencumbered text, I am devoted to a simple, straightforward, and wherever possible, an elegant annotation. An elegant annotation is harder to produce than many people think.

EG. From being editor of a person's letters to being his or her biographer seems a logical step, but it is quite a leap. How do you see the responsibilities of a biographer, and how has Carroll been treated—helped or hurt—by previous biographers? Why do you feel the need to write a life of Carroll?

MC. It is, as you say, quite a step. My own justification for jumping from letter editing to biography starts with my youth, when I began as a creative writer, writing short stories, writing fiction. Even in graduate school, I wanted to stay as close to fiction as I could in my scholarship, and I undertook to write biography for my master's degree and for my Ph.D. dissertation. And indeed, I held the published biography I wrote for my dissertation in my hand when I went up to Columbia to attend commencement at which I got my Ph.D. degree. The copy was for my Ph.D. adviser. That rather unusual happening, having my dissertation published by a commercial house, gave me courage about writing a biography. I really see myself much more as a biographer than an editor of letters.

EG. Are you suggesting that the art of biography is composed of part fiction writing and part letter editing?

MC. No, it is not fiction writing, although Freud would say that—Freud would say that all biographers are liars; one shouldn't believe anything one reads. But I would not say that for a moment. I think that one needs the narrative skill and essential knowledge of dramatic writing in writing biography that one uses in writing fiction. One has to be able to tell one's story if one is going to breathe life into that character. One doesn't make anything up, but one has to be able to assemble the facts and tell them dramatically and in a very lively fashion.

EG. Biography, of course, is a form of interpretation.

MC. Certainly, all history is interpretation. But one must harness oneself; one can do anything in arranging the facts as long as you are faithful to them. That's the ultimate limit.

EG. What stage is your life of Lewis Carroll at?

MC. It's more than half done really. I don't feel that I have to do very much more digging. So much has come into my hands through the search for the letters, and I have kept all that material. I didn't know what I would do with it. I resisted writing the life because I'm the kind of person who likes to move on to other things. I've been with Lewis Carroll very long, and I should really be moving on to someone else. But I think I woke up one morning and said to myself that I just must write the life of Lewis Carroll because I have so much material not available to any other biographer, and a number of the biographers got so much wrong about Lewis Carroll that I feel really I must put my oar into the river as well. I'm not sure that I will write a better biography than the existing ones, but I am sure that there will be information in mine that has never been available before. And that's really why I feel I have to write it.

EG. What is it that you have found that makes you feel compelled to write a new biography?

MC. Well, there are all sorts of things, not only the things one finds, but the connections one makes, that nobody else has made. I wrote a piece on *The Hunting of the Snark* for one of your books, and I made a connection that nobody else had ever made before between the Snark and something mentioned in an unpublished bit of the diaries. It was simply a matter of putting two little things together that happened on the same day. There are dozens if not hundreds of connections like that. We've already spoken of new information in connection with the Liddells; there is still more information along these lines. And I don't think the Carroll connection with the Liddells has been told properly.

EG. Any revelations to be made?

MC. I think there are. You will find that there are later on strong attachments like the Alice attachment that we haven't really hit upon very knowledgeably.

EG. How has Carroll been helped or hurt by previous biographers?

MC. Most biographers usually do help in that they give you insights into the figure they are writing about. And certainly most of Lewis Carroll's biographers have worked well. One or two sloppy workers have jumped to too many conclusions, made illogical leaps, but on the whole I think Carroll has been well served by his biographers, certainly Collingwood, Hudson, and even, I suppose, Mrs. Lennon in her eccentric way. She did an awful lot of work, you know, on that biography and unearthed a good deal of new material, although she makes some leaps that I would renounce. It's her psychological bent that I find unsettling—you know this business of Lewis Carroll being seduced by a gardener when he was a boy. No basis of facts exists there. Also Dr. Greenacre saying there's an unrecorded year in Lewis Carroll's life, and an unrecorded year in anybody's life means that he had a spiritual crisis that year. Now come on! This was when he was at Rugby. Just a busy schoolboy's unrecorded year, you know. There's too much of that sort of thing going on. But on the whole, Hudson and Anne Clark, they have all done good work, and even John Pudney.

108

*EG. Do you know what happened to the missing diaries or the manu-
scripts of his books? Why don't we have many Carroll manuscripts?*

MC. Well, it's all perfectly understandable. The Dodgson family
didn't know the value of the material they had; it just knocked around
in basements and under people's desks. And neglect and carelessness
took their toll.

*EG. Very conscpicuous years of diaries they were careless with,
1858-62.*

MC. Yes, of course, that's what makes one suspicious. That's why
when I wrote that article on the diaries [*The Times,* (London) *Satur-
day Review,* 23 January 1982, p. 9], I suggested that the destruction of
the diaries may have been a deliberate act, at least on one of the
volumes, maybe on all of them that are missing. It could possibly be. I
don't think we shall ever know. We may uncover more material, like
the Wasp piece that has come along; letters are constantly coming in,
as I said. We may learn a lot more about Lewis Carroll. I think there is
a lot more to learn, really. Mine will by no means be the last or
definitive biography. Lots of material will become available.

EG. Manuscripts?

MC. One always hopes. Certainly when I started working on the
Houghton Collection I found manuscripts, things I never dreamed existed, and there they were. And they are much more meaningful than
anyone who has ever held them in their hands ever knew they were.
Take the three "themes" that Carroll composed as an undergraduate
that were erroneously catalogued as "sermons."

*EG. I began by asking you about Carroll's status during the past 20
years; let me close by asking what you think his fate will be over the
next 20 years, or for that matter the next 150.*

MC. I think Carroll will endure in many ways. I think Carroll the man
will endure. He is too interesting for us to lose interest in him as a
man, as a human being. He was gifted. He produced some work that
made us ponder his mind and his unusual quality of imagination. We
constantly strive to come to grips with that imagination. I think that
attempt will continue. And I don't see ourselves writing the last
analysis of that mind in the next twenty years or even in the next 150
years. The works, I think, will endure; as long as there are children on
earth, the *Alice* books will appeal.

DODGSON'S GOLDEN HOURS

Joyce Carol Oates

Editions:

The Pennyroyal Alice: Alice's Adventures in Wonderland, by Lewis
Carroll. Illustrated by Barry Moser. Preface and notes by James R.
Kincaid. Text edited by Selwyn H. Goodacre. West Hatfield,
Massachusetts: Pennyroyal Press, 1982. Limited to 350 copies. 136
pp., extra suite of wood engravings. $1000, out-of-print. (Trade edi-
tion: University of California Press.)

The Hunting of the Snark, by Lewis Carroll. Illustrated by Henry
Holiday. Edited by James Tanis and John Dooley. "The Annotated
Snark" by Martin Gardner. "The Designs for the Snark" by Charles
Mitchell. "The Listing of the Snark" by Selwyn H. Goodacre. Los
Altos, California: William Kaufmann, Inc. in cooperation with Bryn
Mawr College Library, 1981. Subscriber's Edition, x + 129 pp., with
separate portfolio of drawings, $395; Collector's Edition, x + 129
pp., $60; Trade Edition, xc + 129 pp. (with facsimile of first edition),
$18.95.

I

In Charles Lutwidge Dodgson, Oxford clergyman and
Mathematical Lecturer of Christ Church, we have the phenomenon of
the artist "created" by the processes of his own uncanny imagination:
the artist involved in a charming masquerade (in which, at the very
least, two almost distinct personalities co-exist): the artist as suitor, as
swain, as chaste goldhatted lover, a bachelor steadfast in his loyalty
to the child-objects of his adoration but invariably—and necessarily—
betrayed. ("The love of children is a fleeting thing," Dodgson once
observed.) If the inimitable *Alice* books celebrate play within their
frames (that is, in Alice's timeless child-present) and read as elegies
beyond those frames (when, for instance, Alice runs home to tea and
leaves us in the company of her older sister at *Wonderland's* conclusion); if *The Hunting of the Snark: An Agony in Eight Fits* celebrates
loss, madness, violent death, and "soft and sudden vanishing," as
well as the comic impotence of "paper, portfolio, pens, / And ink in
unfailing supplies," it is nevertheless the case that these works are
triumphant affirmations of the will-to-creativity itself, feats of the imagination *sui generis.*

110

One wonders—is "Lewis Carroll" the explicit creation or persona of Charles Dodgson; or is "Lewis Carroll," like the famous works of fiction published under his name, an archetypal expression of the involuntary processes of art?—the unerring selection of memorable images, the instinctive storytelling strategies, the diabolical mastery of what the reader might *will* for art, in compensation for the irresolutions of life. Dodgson is the perennial enigma, Carroll his creation, in the way in which dreams are "our" creations. It was even claimed by observers that the two sides of Dodgson/Carroll's face did not match.

Inventing the first *Alice* book, constructing that most relentlessly artful of poems, the *Snark,* seem to have been primarily a matter of allowing the unconscious to speak. Judging from Dodgson's testimony concerning the events of 4 July 1862, the "invention" of Alice as a fiction had everything to do, and most directly, with the presence of the child Alice Liddell on a rowing expedition from Folly Bridge to Godstow: "Lewis Carroll" is born as Dodgson begins a story plopping his heroine "straight down a rabbit-hole, without the least idea what was to happen afterwards." (The Reverend Robinson Duckworth, a fellow of Trinity, later recalled the remarkable circumstances of that expedition: "The story was actually composed and spoken *over my shoulder* for the benefit of Alice Liddell. I remember turning round and saying, 'Dodgson, is this an extemporary romance of yours?' And he replied, 'Yes, I'm inventing as we go along.' I remember how, when we had conducted the three children back to the Deanery, Alice said, as she bade us good-night, 'Oh, Mr. Dodgson, I wish you would write out Alice's Adventures for me!' . . .")[1] As for the composition of the *Snark,* has any work, "nonsensical" or otherwise, sprung from a less likely source?—

I was walking on a hillside, alone, one bright summer day, when suddenly there came into my head one line of verse—one solitary line—"For the Snark *was* a Boojum, you see." I knew not what it meant, then: I know not what it means, now; but I wrote it down: and, some time afterwards, the rest of the stanza occurred to me, that being its last line: and so by degrees, at odd moments during the next year or two, the rest of the poem pieced itself together, that being its last stanza.[2]

(Dodgson is forty-two years old on this July afternoon in 1874, by now "Lewis Carroll," the famous author of the *Alice* books.) There is no reason to believe Dodgson excessively modest, or disingenuous, in his pronounced use of the passive voice (". . . the poem *pieced itself together*"). The animistic nature of Alice's underground and looking-

[1]See Derek Hudson's *Lewis Carroll: An Illustrated Biography,* 2nd ed. (London: Constable; New York: Clarkson N. Potter, Inc., 1976), pp. 113-115.
[2]"Alice on the Stage," *The Theatre,* April 1887, rpt. in *The Lewis Carroll Picture Book,* ed. Stuart Dodgson Collingwood (London: Unwin, 1899); rpt. as *Diversions and Digressions of Lewis Carroll* (New York: Dover, 1961), p. 165.

glass worlds as well as the fluidity with which creatures metamorphose into one another, or into "lifeless" objects, must have been a metaphoric expression of Dodgson's own spontaneity. For this is the real thing, the primitive and unmistakable flow of the unconscious as it exerts pressure upon consciousness, demanding translation into langauge or images (Dodgson also drew with an inspired amateur's skill). It is simply not the case, as Humpty Dumpty so brashly states, that one can make words mean what he chooses, that one can be "master" of language—or of anything. The dream eventually dissolves. The Bellman tingles his pitiless bell.

The *Alice* books and the *Snark* constitute unique literary experiments in their employment of the elements—the trappings, one might say—of a didactic and resolutely pious Victorian sensibility in the service of an anarchic imagination. The mythopoetics of doubleness of that fascinating era (Dr. Jekyll and Mr. Hyde, Dorian Gray and his "miraculous" portrait come immediately to mind, as well as Dodgson/Carroll) allows a fictional underground or looking-glass world in which formal balance is thwarted repeatedly,[3] logic and commonsense are always suspended, and the disorienting fact is not that most people are mad but that they appear to be quite content in that condition. (The question *Why?* is answered curtly by *Why not?*—the supreme epigram of the dream-world, as it is very likely the supreme epigram of "our" world.) Riddles without answers are more pointedly riddles than riddles *with* answers; dream-figures are uncivil and "rude" (Alice is always recoiling from rudeness) because they speak as they think, in a single gesture. A game like the famous Caucus Race violates our expectations of what a "game" should be (*"Everybody* has won, and *all* must have prizes"—"But who is to give the prizes?"), however humanitarian and even Christian it seems. The significance of tea-time rapidly diminishes if it is *always* tea-time, and the dirty cups and saucers are never changed. One may be obliged to run very rapidly in order to keep one's place, in the Looking-Glass world, or go backwards in order to go forwards; whatever solutions or answers are provided, one can be assured that they will trickle through the head "like water through a sieve." And so on, and so forth: Dodgson's images and metaphors are always brilliant. Above all we are haunted by the sense of a conterminous but invisible "real" world

[3]Alice alone of Wonderland's inhabitants insists upon the need for rules, answers, conclusions, ways of behaving, ends. She brings a pristine "rationalist's" expectations to a thoroughly irrational world: it is she who hopes for a conclusion to the Mouse's pitiable tale, she who complains that the croquet players don't "play at all fairly." Alice's resistance to the counter-logic of Wonderland makes her both a comic and a sympathetic figure, and a recognizable "heroine."

to which the *Alice* books and the *Snark*—including their illustrations by Tenniel, Holiday, and contemporary artists like Barry Moser—provide a sort of hallucinatory mirror.

Dodgson's moods are playful, maddening, elegiac. It has been remarked that Alice is solitary, despite the carnival busyness of her narratives, and it is certainly the case that the poor child has every reason to be thoughtful. For *eating* and *being eaten* are major preoccupations of the books, as many a commentator has noted. DRINK ME to shut up like a telescope, to a height of ten inches—which arouses some natural anxiety in Alice for, after all, it might end "in my going out altogether, like a candle. I wonder what I should be like then?" EAT ME: to open out like the largest telescope that ever was, neck elongated as a swan's: whereupon one is mistaken for the serpent-predator one actually is. The Walrus and the Carpenter devour their trusting oyster charges, and Looking-Glass insects like the Bread-and-butterfly have a hard time of it in the Darwinian struggle for survival. This particular reader, as a very young child, found most terrifying the conclusion of the Looking-Glass feast when all that has been systematically denied becomes possible—becomes manifest. Madness is given a spin of logic. Candles rise to the ceiling, bottles take on plates and forks for limbs, the nightmare is nearly uncontrollable when Alice discovers that the guests are about to be eaten by their "food":

At this moment she heard a hoarse laugh at her side, and turned to see what was the matter with the White Queen, but, instead of the Queen, there was the leg of mutton sitting in a chair. "Here I am!" cried a voice from the soup tureen, and Alice turned again, just in time to see the Queen's broad, good-natured face grinning at her for a moment over the edge of the tureen, before she disappeared into the soup. There was not a moment to be lost. Already several of the guests were lying down in the dishes, and the soup ladle was walking up the table toward Alice's chair, and beckoning to her impatiently to get out of its way.[4]

Since these are children's tales, however, the final triumph is Alice's: she defeats the looking-glass world (and cannibalism), and the rapacious adults of Wonderland (who are "nothing but a pack of cards") simply by waking up. She wakes from her dreams; she saves herself, or is saved, by returning to the "sane" world that encloses and defines the nightmare. *Eating* and *being eaten* may be facts of life in the daytime world, but these facts will be withheld from a child's consciousness, just as the unchecked passion of certain female figures—the Red Queen, the Duchess—submits to a tactful Victorian repression. In Wonderland's courtroom rules are invented on the spot

[4]All quotations to *Alice's Adventures in Wonderland* are cited from *The Pennyroyal Alice* (1982) and later all quotations from *The Hunting of the Snark* are from Martin Gardner's revised *The Annotated Snark* (1981).

and sentences are pronounced first, verdicts afterward: if this is a "fact" of Victorian society it need not impress itself upon girls like Alice. (As Dodgson frankly said, concerning *Alice's* probable audience: "My own idea is, that it isn't a book POOR children would much care for.") Alice's vertiginous changes of size and her frequently expressed fears of becoming extinguished will be postponed altogether, for they are scarcely concerns childhood can accommodate. In *Wonderland* Alice is imagined in the sketchy concluding frame as a "grown woman" who "would keep, through all her riper years, the simple and loving heart of her childhood"—a somewhat perfunctory gesture on Dodgson's part, since the older, *riper* Alice is hardly the Alice he wants to honor and immortalize. In *Looking-Glass*'s similarly conventional frame the child Alice (now more conspicuously a "child" than she was in her turbulent dream) plays with her kitten, and quizzes it on the knotty philosophical issue of who might be dreaming whom—but the danger of the Red King's awakening and Alice's subsequent extinction is clearly past.

Since she never dissolves into helpless tears and is never paralyzed by terror we know that Alice is not a real child but a fantasy-child, a heroine: as Robert Graves has said, "the prime heroine of our nation." Her resourcefulness, her unfailing curiosity, her rationalist spirit and her instinctive sense of fair play and justice make her "ours" in a way that is immensely satisfying to both children and adults, so that Dodgson's early title for *Wonderland—Alice's Golden Hours*—is not altogether inappropriate.

By contrast, *The Hunting of the Snark: An Agony in Eight Fits* has a distinctive—indeed, an obsessive—voice, but no consciousness at its center. Whoever is telling the tale quietly informs us of the disastrous results of the hunt, just as he, or it, informed Dodgson on his afternoon stroll in 1874, a nonsensical conclusion—"For the Snark *was* a Boojum, you see"—that doesn't altogether accommodate the horrific episodes that have transpired. Henry Holiday's extraordinary illustrations for the *Snark,* so literal and meticulous in detail, so serenely mad over-all, are the perfect expression of the *Snark's* voice: distant, detached, occasionally mock-"intimate," knowing, bemused: a voice in a sense *outside the frame,* seeing past and future with equal effortlessness, and acknowledging, unlike the narrative voice of the *Alice* books, not the slightest sympathy with his subject. Alice is always protected by Lewis Carroll's love; the adult men of the Snark expedition—and that Beaver said to be of dubious gender[5]—are on

[5]A small controversy has arisen over the Beaver's precise sex: "he," "she," and "it" have been variously proposed. See Gardner's amusing note in *The Annotated Snark* (1981), p. 15, n. 53.

their own. The Snark is one of those chimerical figures upon which we are invited to project any number of meanings, just as the doomed crew of Ahab's *Pequod* see many things in Moby Dick, including a prodigious quantity of blubber. (Hence theories have been advanced identifying the Snark hunt with the quest for material wealth, social advancement, business success in general; and the philosopher Ferdinand Canning Scott Schiller ingeniously argued, in a parody issue of *Mind* of 1901,[6] that Dodgson was satirizing the Hegelian philosopher's circumlocutory search for the Absolute.) Despite such quasi-rational explanations the *Snark* as a reading or listening experience is unmistakable in its pessimism and cruelty—the obverse of Carroll/Dodgson's sentimentality, perhaps. Since there is no innocent center of consciousness in the midst of the obsessed Snark hunters there is no one fated to survive, save perhaps the Bellman, or the maddening sound of his bell; the final lines belong to the bodiless narrator, and to no one within the poem. The mockery of the conclusion is underscored by its very mildness of expression.

The Hunting of the Snark pitilessly addresses itself to those adults for whom "golden afternoons" are but an intrusive memory, for these are the men—surely Dodgson's satire *is* aimed against masculinity?—who have given up their souls in the Snark-hunt. (Seeking it with thimbles, care, forks, hope; threatening its life with a "railway-share"; charming it—evidently to no avail—with "smiles and soap.") Children are innocent and immortal, adults are fallen and mortal, and one may as well make jokes at their expense, as Balzac and Dickens had done as well. (Though it seems clear that the ballad is innocently nonsensical in its opening stanzas, all play and improvised drollery, until, perhaps, the revelation concerning the Butcher, which is reminiscent of Alice's *faux-pas* involving her cat Dinah, in the opening pages of *Wonderland*.)

If the *Snark* seems to gain power as it proceeds, this is a consequence of the outrageous distance between the ballad's fatuous jangling rimes and the grim story it actually tells us. In the seventh fit the Banker goes mad, or suffers a stroke, or undergoes a witty sort of reversal (like a photographic negative—black where white should be) in these childlike intonations:

> He was black in the face, and they scarcely could trace
>   The least likeness to what he had been:
> While so great was his fright that his waistcoat turned white—
>   A wonderful thing to be seen!

---

[6] "A Commentary on the *Snark*," by Snarkophilus Snobbs. An almost too prodigious parody of *Snark*-hunting, symbol-hunting, and the predicament of "Humanity in search of the Absolute." For Lewis Carroll, like Falstaff, is not only witty in himself but the cause of wit—albeit often a rather strained wit—in others.

> To the horror of all who were present that day,
> He uprose in full evening dress,
> And with senseless grimaces endeavored to say
> What his tongue could no longer express.

(One notes in passing the eerie detachment of "a wonderful thing *to be seen*.")

Yet the hunt for the Snark increases in frenzied zeal, and in the final fit, the eighth, an already nameless hunter, the Baker (variously called "Thingumbob," "Fritter my wig," "What-was-his-name") vanishes before his comrades' eyes:

> They gazed in delight, while the Butcher exclaimed
> "He was always a desperate wag!"
> They beheld him—their Baker—their hero unnamed—
> On the top of a neighbouring crag,
>
> Erect and sublime, for one moment of time.
> In the next, that wild figure they saw
> (As if stung by a spasm) plunge into a chasm,
> While they waited and listened in awe.

The Baker's exclamation fades to absolute silence. And not a button, or feather, or mark remains of him afterward:

> In the midst of the word he was trying to say,
> In the midst of his laughter and glee,
> He had softly and suddenly vanished away—
> For the Snark *was* a Boojum, you see.

It has not been a piece of irrelevant information, that the Snark always looks grave at a pun.

II

The Pennyroyal Alice with its handsome half-leather binding and its outsized (11 x 17 inches) pages is a superb production over-all, though lovers of *Alice*—would they be lovers otherwise?—may have some minor objections. What strikes the eye immediately are Barry Moser's remarkable wood-engravings, which press upon the seasoned reader a new and subtle interpretation of *Alice:* one for adults, perhaps, in which Alice's loneliness is emphasized. We cannot comfortably *see* Alice in this edition, we must *see with* Alice; we must even *become* her, experiencing Wonderland's distortions close up. It is Moser's convincing point that previous *Alice* illustrators, beginning with Carroll himself and including Tenniel, Rackham, Steadman, Pogany, Furniss, and Dali, have "intruded upon the privacy of Alice's adventure, standing apart and observing Alice in her dream. They have been voyeurs, and yet there can be no voyeurs to dreams. . . ." Consequently the artist has composed striking images for us to experience *from within*—except in the book's frame, where we view Alice and her sister, and, in what is surely the most haunting wood-engraving in the series, a vision of Alice Liddell as experienced by Charles Dodgson himself on that memorable midsummer day of 1862 when "Alice" was born. Seemingly posed in a rowboat, this Alice is clearly based upon Dodgson's celebrated photograph, but his inspiration seems to have been French Symbolist. Here is the child-muse as a vampire or chimera out of a dream-canvas by Khnopff, Delville, or Lévy-Dhurmer—the Alice whom Dodgson may very well have seen in his mind's eye. Since, however, the artist's imagination is as rich, undulating, and unfathomable, it seems, as Dodgson's, this single engraving is even more mysterious than a cursory examination will reveal. But readers must make their own discoveries.

Footnotes in the book's page margins are not only discreetly placed, in attractive red ink, but the more commendable for being so spare, and so unfailingly interesting. (A god's eye of scholarship and criticism pertaining to Lewis Carroll is provided for us in James Kincaid's succinct, graceful prose.) Though in his preface, Kincaid advances what is surely a debatable theory regarding Alice's character—that she is a "mini-adult" and finally "ineducable," being resistant to the "liberation that anarchy offers, unable to enter into a world of free-play." Mr. Kincaid's first-hand experience with "free-play" of the sort taking place in Wonderland ("Off with his head!" "Off with her head!") isn't suggested in his text, and one suspects that his experience with that "quaint" value Anarchy is a dictionary experience solely. In any case it is highly unlikely that *Alice's Adventures in Wonderland* celebrates a child's movement "with disastrous ease into the prison-house of adulthood," leaving behind a "melancholy, glorious dream": the simplest experience of *reading* the story insists otherwise. Alice triumphs, and she triumphs over a pack of rather murderous "mini-adults" who could not be considered by any generous stretch of the imagination "educators."

Though I am no admirer of Monotype Bembo with its fussy and distracting ligatures, the general appearance of the book is exemplary, and the subtle employment of various inks—blue, red, even a sparing gold—an inspired idea. One is tempted to say that the *Pennyroyal Alice* is worth the penny at which it is priced—an ideal collector's item.

This weighty morocco-edged edition of *The Hunting of the Snark* is nearly as appealing an example of book production as the *Alice*. It is a veritable cornucopia for *Snark*-people, bringing together in one

sibility in printing the "cheap" version of the poem without the idiosyncratic Dickinson punctuation?)

These are, however, minor observations, which will not discourage serious collectors from the book. One might in fact note in passing that the edition's outstanding features—the fascinating preliminary drawings for the *Snark,* here published for the first time, and Charles Mitchell's lengthy, meticulous, and illuminating essay on the drawings—are nearly worth the price of the Collector's Edition alone.

SHE'S ALL MY FANCY PAINTED HIM

Robert Dupree

Biography:

Lewis Carroll: A Biography. By Anne Clark. London: J. M. Dent; New York: Schocken Books, 1979. 288 pp.

The Letters of Lewis Carroll. Edited by Morton N. Cohen with the assistance of Roger Lancelyn Green. London: Macmillan; New York: Oxford University Press, 1979. 2 vols. xxxviii, 614 pp. and viii, (615)-1245 pp.

Lewis Carroll, Photographer of Children: Four Nude Studies. With an introduction by Morton N. Cohen. Philadelphia: The Philip H. & A. S. W. Rosenbach Foundation, 1978; New York: Clarkson N. Potter, 1979. 32 pp.

Lewis Carroll and the Kitchins. Edited by Morton N. Cohen. New York: The Lewis Carroll Society of North America and The Argosy Bookshop, 1980. xvi, 48 pp.

And Selected Biographical Essays.

"The great strategic difficulty of biography," according to A. O. J. Cockshut, is the "conflict between evidence and interpretation."[1] This problem is nowhere better exemplified than in the bumper crop of biographical studies of Lewis Carroll that appeared in 1979 and continues in a steady harvest of new information. Never before has so much evidence been available to the reading public. Yet the massive amount of material that is gradually becoming accessible to Carroll scholars poses problems of its own. Many of the strategies for dealing with Carroll's life will have to be reconceived as old surmise is replaced by new evidence requiring new interpretations.

Though Carlyle once referred to the "unspeakable delight" that men take in reading about others' lives, most biographies from the Victorian era seem less provocative of delight than of impatience. Lytton Strachey's famous description of them as two fat volumes consisting of masses of material assembled without design is fairly accurate. Certainly the typical *Life and Letters* of a great man was supposed to engage its readers directly, independent of any interpretative intermediary. In *Contarini Fleming* Disraeli spoke of the superiority of biography—life without theory, to history—life explicated accord-

---

[1] *Truth to Life: The Art of Biography in the Nineteenth Century* (New York: Harcourt Brace Jovanovich, 1974), p. 10.

ing to some preconceived scheme. The mass of letters, speeches, diaries, and miscellaneous "remains" were supposed to speak for themselves. Unfortunately, the material was seldom as straightforward as this ideal suggests. Many an eminent Victorian managed to destroy the evidence of things unseen when he wished them to remain that way. As a result, these landmarks of nineteenth-century greatness often shine more with the gleam of the bonfire than with the light of revelation.

Many of Lewis Carroll's personal papers were destroyed in ignorance of their future value. Other unpublished writings, such as the diaries, were edited with a razor by family members even more concerned with privacy than their unusually scrupulous relative. Yet Carroll himself seems to have had no concern about revelations after his death. The only holocausts he ordered were for materials that might embarrass others, such as his photographs of nude children. Privacy was a convenience he sought while alive, it is true. Isa Bowman tells how "despite his love for the photographer's art, he hated the idea of having his own picture taken for the benefit of a curious world. The shyness that made him nervous in the presence of strangers made the idea that any one who cared to stare into a shop window could examine and criticise his portrait extremely repulsive to him."[2] This "shyness" did not extend to matters beyond the grave, it seems, for unlike T. S. Eliot, Carroll left no directions in his will discouraging biographies. He never attempted, as Henry James did, to destroy evidence or hint at its existence while covering the traces in order to make life miserable for his future biographers. He trusted in—but only partly received—the discretion of his survivors.

Stuart Collingwood produced a first account of his uncle's life with astonishing speed after Carroll's death. It is a primary source of information that will never be completely superceded, but it is also much more. Though Langford Reed criticized it for lacking an organizing theory, Collingwood's version of his uncle's life has had a great—if unrecognized—impact on all subsequent accounts. As Cockshut points out (p. 18), Victorian biographies have almost nothing to say about the childhood of their subjects: "We learn very fully what a man thought between fifty and sixty when his attitudes changed little, and hardly anything of what he thought between ten and twenty when they changed much." What is unusual about Collingwood's *Life and Letters of Lewis Carroll* is its emphasis on the childhood of Charles Dodgson. This detailed account of his uncle's very early years is a striking departure from the tradition of Victorian biography. It is

[2]*The Story of Lewis Carroll* (London: J. M. Dent, 1899), p. 11.

made even more remarkable by the author's inclusion of a whole chapter on Carroll's child-friends. This change of emphasis from heroic maturity to childlike innocence reflects a radical shift in sensibility that shaped or even determined the ways in which Carroll's life would be viewed by succeeding generations of biographers. Collingwood's book is not, then, simply an indispensable mine of information; it is a radical reinterpretation of greatness.

As a source of information, Anne Clark's biography of Lewis Carroll is a worthy successor to Collingwood's. It is well organized and thorough. The author draws on a number of neglected sources that illuminate not only Carroll's character but also the nature of the world he inhabited. She provides details neglected by others, such as the sort of reading that the Dodgson children were exposed to at an early age. Her close association with the Lewis Carroll Society allows her to stay abreast of the latest discoveries, and she has assembled most of them in this volume. Where she is strongest is in providing background for Carroll's academic years, particularly during those times when he was involved in the never-ending crises and controversies engendered by the reform movement. It is regrettable that this very useful book appeared so soon after Derek Hudson's revised version of his own life of Lewis Carroll and so near in time to Morton Cohen's forthcoming one. The result is that this biography is bound to seem transitional in nature, serving mainly to update and round out the picture of Carroll that has been emerging for the last two decades.

The most telling feature of Anne Clark's biography is an almost strenuous avoidance of interpretation. The view of Carroll offered in her pages is sympathetic and unfailingly generous, but it has no overarching theme that allows one to see what kind of story he is telling. Her refusal to theorize is understandable, perhaps, in view of the treatments of Carroll that have preceded hers. Langford Reed's version of him as Dr. Jekyll and Mr. Hyde, Florence Becker Lennon's emphasis on escapism and bitterness at the heart of his laughter, and Phyllis Greenacre's story of confused sexual identity emerging from a disrupted early childhood have never found much favor in England. Later Carroll biographers, such as R. L. Green and Derek Hudson, have been openly contemptuous of what they regard as arbitrary Freudian interpretation. Nevertheless, even Hudson is willing to speak of a man who never outgrew his childhood and remained "fixated" on his early years. Anne Clark seems determined not to interpret where the evidence is too slender; it is possible, however, that her praiseworthy caution goes too far in the other direction.

There is a barely discernible theme in Clark's story; it is sounded at the very beginning. Carroll's father, she suggests, had the "raw material of genius" and could have become "a literary giant." What follows is a clear rebuff to those who speak of a disorderly childhood that later caused some psychic disruption. Clark sees the source of Carroll's unique genius in the congenial household that nurtured him. His was simply the pre-eminent expression of a talent shared by many members of his family. If this is indeed the interpretative strategy of Anne Clark's biography, it is a pity that she does not make her point of view more explicit. The idea deserves a more intensive discussion.

Morton Cohen's vigorous editorial labors have also added considerably to our stock of information about Lewis Carroll. His handsome edition of the letters in a two-volume, boxed set is the first attempt at a comprehensive collection of the correspondence. It was long overdue. This is not, however, a complete collection; of the more than four thousand letters Cohen has located, he presents slightly under a third here. The selection must have been difficult, and on the whole it is even-handed and, within the imposed limits, very intelligent. This is not a publication like the Yale edition of Walpole's letters, which is primarily of interest to scholars and historians. It is obviously meant to appeal to a fairly wide audience, even if the scholarly standards are certainly very high. Those writing on certain areas of Carroll's life will regret the absence of much correspondence concerning affairs at Oxford, the give-and-take between author and publisher or illustrator, and theatrical matters. Cohen has been careful to note these and other sacrifices in his preface, and he tries to print some representative samples of each category. It is difficult to criticize his decisions, since, after all, how many of us have seen as much Carrolliana as he?

Some of the correspondence that was excluded because it did not have the kind of broad appeal that this sort of presentation demands may have its own importance. Cohen's supplement to his collection in the form of a very attractive volume of Carroll's letters to the Kitchins demonstrates what is lost and what gained in the process of selection. The letters became available to Cohen only after he had completed his larger edition, and they contain no great surprises. The reader looking for more of the kind of brilliance that Carroll displays at his best will be disappointed. Even so, there is useful information about Carroll the photographer and, above all, about his relationship with close friends. He admired and approved of the work of G. W. Kitchin, had a relaxed and occasionally collaborative relationship with Mrs. Kitchin, and held their daughter Xie in high esteem as a photographic model. The correspondence with the Kitchins would have been lost among the letters of the collected edition. Here it tells an interesting story and actually gains by being presented in isolation. Cohen's annotations also provide extremely valuable insights into a family interesting in its own right.

Lewis Carroll's skill as a photographer was given important recognition by historian of photography Helmut Gernsheim. Cohen's study of Carroll as photographer of nude children is a very valuable supplement to Gernsheim's book; equally important, it offers some corrections. Carroll's pictures of nude children were long thought to have perished so utterly that not a single example survived. This book provides four excellent specimens, which at one point were colored and given a mounting that suggests how much they were prized. Along with the single example in Graham Ovenden's *Victorian Children* (if it is authentic), these are a direct basis for judging Carroll's most controversial activity. Cohen does not deny that Mrs. Grundy was a frequent problem, but he refuses to see anything voyeuristic about the "favorite dress of nothing." He also shows convincingly that Carroll's decision to stop photographing could not have been the result of a scandal, as Gernsheim claimed. Victorian iconography made baroque putti and naked angel-children a familiar sight in public buildings and churches. Child nudity was practiced routinely on beaches. Carroll found in the nude figure of the child an image of freshness and purity, according to Cohen, a lovely innocence that was naturally close to God. He was scrupulous about avoiding any offense or guilt for child or parent. It may be we, rather than Carroll, who are the victims of anachronistic and puritanical suspicions.

Cohen announces in the introduction to his edition of the correspondence that the remaining letters will eventually appear in separate volumes. He also promises that the identification and location of all the letters, an essential scholarly task, will be published. One assumes that he will have a large hand in these projects and will continue to provide the same detailed and thoughtful annotations that characterize his editing so far. Even when the letters are accessible to scholars, the information contained in them will be incomplete if they are not well indexed and annotated. Cohen often goes beyond this minimal courtesy to his reader, offering interesting sidelights and learned allusions that demonstrate his genuine seriousness about the value of Carroll's writings. At one point, for instance, he notes that Carroll shared with that great humanist John Milton a confusion about the names of the Fates and those of the Furies. The annotations are themselves an important mine of information about Carroll's contemporaries, and they help challenge the usual image of him as an interesting writer but a rather dull person. This and other work by Cohen is destined to force a reassessment of the man as well as of the writings.

An excellent illustration of how such a reinterpretation can come about is contained in Cohen's article "Lewis Carroll and the House of Macmillan" (*Browning Institute Studies* 7 [1979], 31-70), where he surveys the exchange of letters between author and publisher. In the course of this account, we learn that much of our impression of Carroll as unreasonably difficult is lacking in foundation. After a careful examination of Victorian publishing practice, Cohen concludes that the relationship between Carroll and Macmillan reflects "not so much the nature of the man as the nature of the terms between author and publisher." He goes further: "Dodgson clearly realized that, through the years, he had made extraordinary demands upon Macmillan & Co., but they surely realized, in turn, that he was an extraordinary person and author." As in his more recent "The Actress and the Don: Ellen Terry and Lewis Carroll" (in *Lewis Carroll: A Celebration,* pp. 1-14, reviewed elsewhere in this collection), Cohen shows that a careful examination of the evidence refutes the accepted or popular interpretation. His own forthcoming biography, to judge from the articles he has published so far, will offer a number of such correctives.

A truly distinguished biography of Lewis Carroll has yet to be published. Whether or not Cohen's interpretation of the life will produce an account of the first rank remains to be seen; the whole story of a life is not the same as the scattered insights a scholar may produce from separate episodes and themes. Indeed, Carroll's life appears to the prospective biographer to be not unlike the great hall in Wonderland. There are many passages to the truth about his character, but only one door will lead us to understand what Carroll saw in his most profound moments. He saw the lovely garden just beyond the tiny door that opened onto his principal insight into human nature, and the key to that door was Alice. Like Cervantes and his Quixote, the two are inseparable in our imaginations, and the biographer must recognize that his account of the author will always be affected by his picture of that relationship. Anne Clark puts forth a somewhat hesitant suggestion that Carroll did indeed want to marry Alice. Cohen has asserted the possibility rather more boldly in a recent article for *The Times* (January 23, 1982, p. 9). If they are correct, then much of the psychoanalytical interpretation of Carroll will have to be reconsidered. Alice certainly becomes a more comprehensible figure in his life—the person who led him to two important truths: the meaning of love and the positive benefits of personal renunciation, the main themes of *Sylvie and Bruno.* The historical Alice, as Anne Clark's new biography of her almost unwittingly reveals (*The Real Alice: Lewis Carroll's Dream Child,* London: Michael Joseph, 1982), led an uninteresting life as an adult. But the "dream child" was Carroll's

Beatrice and Laura. He was the last of the courtly lovers, and the ritual courtship he enacted over and over again was not the product of an obsession or even a form of compensation for a lost fulfilment. It was a way of life that he discovered through Alice, a kind of purification rite that led him, like Dante and Petrarch, to a sense of some higher reality.

Whether or not such an interpretation of their relationship is tenable, it is at least clear that Alice is unlike any of Carroll's other protagonists, for she is by turns audience, heroine, and storyteller. At the end of *Alice's Adventures in Wonderland,* the author releases her to the world to recount her dream, to become a future transmitter of his and her story. At the conclusion of *Through the Looking-Glass,* where she anticipates her role as mother, she is also allowed to wonder about the character of her identity. Is she a character in the Red King's dream or he a character in hers? Both Alice and Lewis Carroll are characters in a story—his, hers, and ours.

Lewis Carroll obviously taught Alice something, but what did he learn from her? Perhaps the disappointment of not being allowed to marry her led to the theme that is repeated so frequently in his writings: life is a dream; don't look for perfect joy in this world; learn to renounce your selfish desires and devote yourself to the happiness of others. This choice could lead in the end to an even greater happiness for yourself. *Sylvie and Bruno* embodies that philosophy, but, alas, must be a story without the real Alice. Nevertheless, shouldn't Carroll be taken at his word? Is it not possible that he meant what he said, that he knew what he was about and consciously repressed certain feelings in order to move to higher goals? Even if this sketch of an interpretation of Lewis Carroll's life is itself too fanciful to be supported by the evidence, it does point to the need for a new way of seeing Lewis Carroll as possessing a comprehensible mind with clear and conscious motives, a healthy mind that coped with disappointment in a positive and fruitful fashion and left the world a little better for his sorrows. Anne Clark's and Morton Cohen's work may or may not give us a definitive Lewis Carroll, but their biographical and editorial efforts will certainly force us to entertain some new notions about who he was.

THE CARROLLIAN PAPERCHASE

Peter Heath

Bibliography:

The Lewis Carroll Handbook. By S. H. Williams and F. W. Madan, Revised by R. L. Green, Further Revised by Denis Crutch. Folkestone, England: Dawson; Hamden, Connecticut: Archon Books, 1979. xix, 340 pp.

Lewis Carroll: An Annotated International Bibliography, 1960-77. By Edward Guiliano. Charlottesville: University Press of Virginia; Brighton, England: Harvester Press, 1980. viii, 253 pp.

Lewis Carroll and Alice, 1832-1982. By Morton N. Cohen. New York: Pierpont Morgan Library, 1982. 133 pp.

Lewis Carroll's Library. Edited and Introduced by Jeffrey Stern. (Carroll Studies No. 5) Charlottesville: Lewis Carroll Society of North America and the University Press of Virginia, 1981. xiv, 95 pp.

The main problems of Carroll bibliography are primarily created by Carroll himself. A compulsive busybody and fusspot, who unfortunately had all-too-ready access to printing facilities, he abused the press in much the same way that an overactive modern academic abuses his photocopy machine. Every notion or project which entered that busy, pernickety mind was no sooner committed to paper than it was rushed off to the printer, to be reproduced as a circular in ten, fifty or a couple of hundred copies, depending on how many other people it was intended to pester on the subject. And since nothing was ever got right the first time, the same piece would soon after reappear in revised and amended versions, so that an opuscule of absolutely no importance in the first place winds up floating about in half-a-dozen different states and "editions," to be duly scavenged by collectors and solemnly catalogued by bibliographers, as if it were a serious literary product of the master's pen. Only Lenin and Stalin, among modern authors, have been exposed by their idolators to the same sort of indiscriminate rubbish-collecting; it would have been better for all three if an agreement had long ago been made to exclude such stuff as not genuine publication, not part of their literary output, instead of allowing it to choke and clutter the record, as it does to this very day.

Part cause and part victim of the process, the *Lewis Carroll Handbook,* now in its fourth revision, is a sad example of what happens when enthusiasts attempt to keep tally of the Dodgson papyrology, and make no effort to separate it from the genuinely published work. The successive compilers, S. H. Williams, F. W. Madan, R. L. Green, and now Denis Crutch, all were or are men of learning, unable to resist gossipping and digressing about their little discoveries, so that what started as a mere check-list has ballooned over the years into a rambling, ill-proportioned ragbag of Carrollian lore and speculation, whose contents, though not unamusing to read, are of little use to anyone, and of virtually no relevance to the original purposes of the work. The mania for including everything that Dodgson ever printed has gradually spread to manuscript trivia subsequently published by others, and to the recording of conjectural items, merely alluded to in the *Diaries,* or reported by Collingwood, the first biographer, though their existence as printed pieces has never been confirmed by any other evidence at all. Carroll has only to mention that he cobbled up a song for some wretched children's theatricals at Eastbourne, and down it goes in the *Handbook* as an apparently *bona fide* entry, though nobody has set eyes on it from that day to this. Fugitive scraps that survive only as dog-eared single sheets in the Parrish Collection at Princeton (the *Handbook*'s main kitchen-midden) are likewise treated as authentic publications, though everything indicates that they were no such thing. The *Handbook* is full of such dubious padding, born of a deep-seated confusion about what *constitutes* publication, and is thus a misleading and tiresome work for the ordinary Carroll student to consult. To find what you want, you have to plough through a morass of pedantic fribble and ill-assorted typography; by the time you get there, you have generally forgotten what you were looking for in the first place.

These faults are not new, of course, and Mr. Crutch can be condemned only for the timidity of his efforts to remedy them, and for failing to make the extent of his own interventions clear. He has also done little to overcome the notorious parochialism of the original—American work seems hardly to count unless it is republished in Britain—or its snobbish indifference to the interests of those who are *not* papyrologists, or collectors of expensive waste-paper, and whose ambitions extend no further, say, than to the acquisition of translations or twentieth-century illustrated editions of the major works. In the earlier versions, there used to be inadequate but still useful hand-lists of ephemera and translations. They have now disappeared—to save space, allegedly—with barely a word of apology or regret. The tables (which survive) of "ordinary" English and American *Alice*s were always contemptibly amateurish, being full of mistakes and misprints and lacunae that a little research (or even ordinary carefulness) could easily have served to rectify. Here, at least, was an opportunity for the new editor to do something useful, but alas, he has failed to take it. Apart from the perfunctory addition of a few titles, nothing has been altered—not even the misprints. So feeble a recension of a work already in decrepitude is really no service to the Carroll public, and reflects but little glory upon English Carroll scholarship. The best that can be said of it—as of hay when feeling faint—is that there is still nothing like it. But that, as the White King noted, is a long way from saying that there is, or could be, nothing better.

For an example of something better, one turns with relief to Edward Guiliano's *Annotated International Bibliography.* This is a valiant and largely successful attempt to catalogue the spate of Carroll literature that has appeared between 1960 and 1977. As such, it explicitly aims to supplement the deficiencies of the *Handbook,* but its purview, in fact, is far wider. Editions, translations and critical or biographical writings from many languages are included, with enough in the way of annotations to indicate the nature and content of each. The 1500-odd entries are arranged chronologically, under four broad categories, with (unlike the *Handbook*) an efficient system of numbering and cross-referencing, which makes it easy, with a little practice, to find one's way about. The labor of compilation has obviously benefitted from the use of modern systems of information retrieval, and from the help of librarians around the world; but, equally obviously, the editor has not been content with mere tabulation, but has verified everything he could, and foraged actively on his own account. As an example of his diligence, he has effectively drawn up, *en passant,* a much-needed index to the files of *Jabberwocky,* the English Carrollian journal which harbors a fair proportion of the more serious recent research in this area, and for this alone would deserve his readers' thanks. Within the time-span it embraces, the *AIB* can more generally be commended, as a comprehensive, well-arranged and trustworthy work of reference that will be helpful to every Carroll scholar, and to most will be a humiliating revelation of lethargy and ignorance. If it cannot (and does not) claim to have run down absolutely everything, it certainly opens up many an obscure corner of the literature, and conveys, in doing so, a lively sense of the worldwide interest that Carroll now inspires. It is too bad that a work of such virtue should again be marred by misprints—of which "The *Version* of the Three T's," twice in one entry, is perhaps the most culpable; but in all else, Guiliano sets a standard which others can henceforth be called upon to follow. It is much to be hoped that he (or somebody else) will carry this project forward at intervals, and perhaps even backwards as well. For in the absence of a thorough survey, *à la Guiliano,* all the way back to 1898, there is really no knowing how much that was ignored or omitted by the *Handbook* is waiting to be brought to light.

The catalogues of major exhibitions—such as those mounted in London and New York for the centennial celebrations in 1932—can themselves make a useful contribution to bibliography, since they often throw up entries that are not recorded elsewhere. The sesquicentennial exhibit this year, at the Pierpont Morgan Library in New York, was certainly in this class. Based essentially on the celebrated Arthur A. Houghton, Jr. collection, arranged and catalogued by Morton N. Cohen, it displayed many choice and remarkable items, ranging from unique personal memorabilia, through all the more customary rarities, to a selection of those "spin-offs" and ephemera which have seldom been preserved in other collections, and are thus quite probably almost as scarce, in their own way, as the inscribed copies, the first editions, the obscure pamphlets and the famous *UrAlice* manuscript, which formed the centerpiece of the show. Professor Cohen's catalogue is primarily a transcript of his own informative captions, fleshed out with an introductory essay and prefatory notes to each section; as such, it is quite properly directed less to the specialist than to the *profanum vulgus* (who arrived, of course, at 36th Street in unprecedented droves). Since nobody knows more about Carroll, or is a better hand at lucid and graceful exposition of the subject, it goes without saying that anyone who reads through *Lewis Carroll and Alice* will learn a great deal, and be reminded of more, in the most pleasant kind of way. The emphasis, however, is biographical. Professor Cohen, one may surmise, is a good deal more interested in Carroll himself than in the niceties that bedevil the description of his minor works. For the bibliographer, therefore, the gleanings are not all that rich; though as a partial record of the last great American collection to have remained, till now, in its original ownership, this catalogue will obviously retain its importance, at least until a complete listing can be made available.

The fifth in the series of books issued by the Lewis Carroll Society of North America is also a contribution to bibliography, though of a rather different kind. Carroll had a fair-sized library, which was hastily dispersed after his death by an Oxford firm of auctioneers. *Lewis Carroll's Library* reprints in facsimile the catalogue of this sale, together with three other lists that were issued, soon afterwards, by the Oxford booksellers who presumably acquired most of the loot. The point of including them is that they give a better idea of the content of many lots that were carelessly or vaguely described in the auction catalogue itself. Jeffrey Stern, who has assembled this material, gives an interesting account of what happened, but refrains—probably wisely—

from attempting to annotate or discuss the details, though he does provide a partial breakdown, under various categories, in the index. The casual reader is thus left to form his own impression of the range of Dodgson's reading, and to gasp in envy at the ridiculous prices fetched by those minor Carrolliana which nowadays empty the pockets of millionaires. For the specialist, of course, there is a rich mine of queries and enigmas. What has happened, for example, to the handwritten "rough draft" of *Euclid and His Modern Rivals?* If it still survives, it must be just about the only known example of a major Dodgson MS. The chief thing one notices about the list as a whole is that it is more an accumulation of books than a systematic collection. The amount of mathematics and theology in it is not large; the British logicians of the period are fairly well represented; English literature is quite strong, with Scott and Dickens (though not Trollope) among the novelists, and a wide choice of poets, including a number of first editions of the Romantics; the real disappointment is in the children's book section, where the information given is at its most inadequate, precisely at the point of greatest need. Dodgson clearly followed the work of his contemporaries in this area, and even collected his imitators; but for those in search of links and influences, the evidences here are too shaky, and the clues too few, to add much substance to what was already known before.

THREE ALICES, THREE CARROLLS

Kathleen Blake

Criticism:

Lewis Carroll: A Celebration. Edited by Edward Guiliano. New York: Clarkson N. Potter, 1982. 224 pp.

And Selected Criticism, 1976-82.

Lewis Carroll: A Celebration marks "the occasion of the 150th anniversary of the birth of Charles Lutwidge Dodgson" and the second important drawing together of work on Carroll by Edward Guiliano. A review of the range of literary criticism between Guiliano's 1976 *Lewis Carroll Observed* (New York: Potter) and the 1982 volume reveals plenty of activity and some significant developments. I discern three Alices, and can make out three Carrolls as well.

My triad of Alices I call Angst Alice, Malice Alice, and Heiter Alice. These names will take some explaining. They characterize positions that may be generalized beyond attitudes toward Alice herself, and perhaps Guiliano identifies analogous poles of possibility between Angst and Heiterkeit in his "A Time for Humor: Lewis Carroll, Laughter and Despair, and *The Hunting of the Snark.*" While Guiliano reminds us of the laughter in Carroll's works, he gives more stress to dread, nightmare, anxiety, "the pessimism of the *Alice* books," "the horror of the *Snark.*" His fine analysis of the time-haunted figure of the Bellman aligns him with commentators or Carrollian Angst.

Among these, a leading commentator is Donald Rackin. His "Blessed Rage: Lewis Carroll and the Modern Quest for Order" in the *Celebration* volume follows the track of his own 1966 essay ("Alice's Journey to the End of Night," *PMLA,* vol. 81) to trace Alice's exploration of a godless, post-Darwinian, "dark human consciousness," her "doomed human quest for ultimate meaning" amidst the "morally unintelligible void." Rackin recognizes comedy but mostly finds in Wonderland and Looking-Glass the blackness of *The Heart of Darkness.* Anne K. Mellor adds to the tradition of Rackin in her chapter "Fear and Trembling: From Lewis Carroll to Existentialism" in *English Romantic Irony* (Cambridge and London: Harvard Univ. Press, 1980). Finding that Alice and her creator react to the radical irrationality of things with "more anxiety and fear than unmitigated wonder and delight," she notes the proximity of publication dates and concerns between the *Alices* and the writings of Søren Kierkegaard.

While some romantic ironists may exult in the freedom of relativity and find potentiality in the flux of being and meaning, the existentialist does not. Mellor places Carroll's fantasies on the verge of existentialism in their evocation of Angst but finds no redeeming leap of faith in them to match Kierkegaard's. By contrast, Rackin allows for a modicum of affirmation. In the face of Angst, Alice teaches us how to bear life. She chooses to survive, even though she must partly do so by means of lies and spite. Connecting Rackin's interpretation and that of Roger Sale in *Fairy Tales and After: From Snow White to E. B. White* (Cambridge and London: Harvard Univ. Press, 1978) is some awareness of malice in Alice but more admiration for her than for the upsetting world she must confront and leave. Thus Sale finds Alice pettish at times but more decent than anything she meets, rather gallantly if naively refusing to learn the lessons of Looking-Glass that "things never go right, rules don't hold, explanations confuse as much as they explain, and there is never any jam"; she refuses to adjust to a world in which punishments come as a matter of course and the only choice lies in whether or not to commit the crime. Sale lends his attention and eloquence to the White Queen and makes her loom larger than we might expect after much past critical concentration on the Red Queen. The White Queen becomes King Lear. Sale locates the appeal of Carroll's story in its heroine's systems of defense against the anxieties of experience. That is, the work will appeal to those among us (and Sale counts himself out) who are as Angst-prone as Carroll. A further example of the Angst Alice view appears in Robert Pattison's *The Child Figure in English Literature* (Athens, Georgia: Univ. of Georgia Press, 1978). Pattison proposes an elaborate but ultimately too simple and rigid history of attitudes towards childhood. He confines himself to a Christian frame of reference which dictates the alternatives of original sin or original innocence, Augustinian or Pelagian positions. Carroll becomes a "semi-Pelagian." Alice as child enters a realm of adult sin where all lie under sentence of death and Sisyphean punishment by repetition (Tea-Party), where language itself is corrupt. Alice's innocence allows her to defy this world by asserting her faith in a "logician God," yet her escape as a child does not abolish the state of original sin into which adulthood must fall.

As we turn from Angst Alice to Malice Alice we remain within the heart of darkness, for while Wonderland and Looking-Glass brighten up, Alice herself becomes more tainted. She loses innocence and tends to be seen as the adult, the creatures as relative children. She becomes a willful, even authoritarian imposer of order on a benign fantasy anarchy. The touch of malice in Alice, which Sale can excuse and Rackin value, ceases to be found quite endurable or endearing.

According to Terry Otten's "After Innocence, Alice in the Garden" in *A Celebration,* Alice represents a stage of growth *between* innocence and the fall. She is innocent enough to enter the garden, too fallen to avoiding perceiving it in fallen terms. A telling example is her distress at death threats that, after all, never do come to anything in this dream world. Her viewpoint imports Angst into Wonderland and provokes malice against it. Unfitted for the garden, Alice destroys it. There follow paragraphs on her bad character. "She betrays a proclivity for violence, moral tyranny, and unswerving absolutism." She is reductive, holds linear assumptions, circumscribes reality; she deteriorates, becomes a fallen Eve, a serpent. Otten tries to resist condemning Alice altogether, since we must all grow up, but he stresses a nostalgia for lost innocence in Carroll, approaching that of J. M. Barrie's nostalgia for Neverland. This comparison fails of effect since Barrie's own attitude was not so one-sided; he treated the price of growing up *and* the price of remaining a child.

Otten acknowledges the lineage of his ideas from James Kincaid's important 1975 essay ("Alice's Invasion of Wonderland," *PMLA,* vol. 88). In his portraiture of Malice Alice he also owes a great deal to Lionel Morton's interesting "Memory in the Alice Books," *Nineteenth-Century Fiction,* 33 (1978), 285-308. He cites Morton's identification of Alice with the Red Queen, that is, the desire to domineer and punish, to grow up. Morton expresses some other concerns, most provocatively the strange juxtaposition of idealization and forgetfulness of the past in Carroll's work, most controversially the motives for forgetting in Carroll's evasion of "the mother hidden in memory." Marked parallels to Otten's interpretation appear, too, in James Suchan's "Alice's Journey from Alien to Artist," *Children's Literature,* 7 (1978), 78-92. Again, Alice wishes to escape adult boredom and restrictions but finds she cannot accept childish anarchy because she brings adult values with her. Thus she proves both sadist and masochist, injuring the creatures and herself, and grows up to master her experience by destroying it. That is, she becomes the storyteller at the end of *Wonderland* and the conscious creator of the tale of *Looking-Glass.* She transforms the disturbing realities of her experience into accounts of the simple joys of childhood. Here is a more culpable artist-liar than the Alice who let there be light in a dark place, according to Rackin.

One more work with something to say about Malice Alice is Roger B. Henkle's *Comedy and Culture* (Princeton, New Jersey; Guildford, Surrey: Princeton Univ. Press, 1980). Placing Carroll within a Victorian comic tradition, Henkle constructs a tripartite model of comedy: (1) satire against existing conventions, (2) free-play elaboration of alternate worlds, (3) closure, which may be so arbitrary as not really to deny radical alternatives, but which often retreats into conventional values. Lewis Carroll unfortunately favors the latter type of closure. Not so much Alice as Carroll is seen as seeking freedom from Victorian constraint in fantasy. However, unable to enjoy too much of the free-play of Wonderland, he finds anxieties intruding and with them the willful authority figures who multiply in Looking-Glass, leading to a final "self-strangulation" of radical comedy. There is less of malice, perhaps, more of loss of nerve here, but Henkle can be grouped with the others who find something to regret in conclusions that repudiate benignly childish nonsense worlds.

From both Angst and Malice we now take a big step to Heiter Alice, a figure not strongly represented in the *Celebration* volume. Austin Warren's "Carroll and His Alice Books" in *Sewanee Review*, 88 (1980), 331-353, gives me the term Heiterkeit, German for gaiety, cheerful serenity, blitheness without Weltschmertz, the qualities of Mozart, Goethe, Auden in old age. Most of Warren's essay consists of predictable biographical and literary background; yet he strikes a keynote with his Heiter Alice. Warren likes Carroll's heroine and thinks her manners and sanity make her dreams more pleasant than unpleasant.

In his *Lewis Carroll* (Boston: Twayne, 1977) Richard Kelly calls some attention to a presiding spirit of playfulness in Carroll. Much fuller development is provided by Robert M. Polhemous in *Comic Faith: The Great Tradition from Austen to Joyce* (Chicago and London: Chicago Univ. Press, 1980). Like Kelly, Polhemous cites earlier work celebrating the play spirit in Carroll such as my own *Play, Games, and Sport, The Literary Works of Lewis Carroll* (Ithaca and London: Cornell Univ. Press, 1974) and goes further to initiate a history of laughter and to place Carroll within a tradition of "mirth [which] so intensifies the moment that it could be described as sanctifying life." Post-God (and Darwin and Freud) Angst and malice fade from the picture, dark recedes before light, and Polhemous finds faith and vitality. His historical introduction opposes laughter to Christian other-worldliness in revering a natural regeneration in this world. Christianity and comedy achieve rapprochement in Erasmus, Rabelais, Swift, and Sterne, and comic faith fills in more and more for lost dogma in the nineteenth century. This is all pretty sketchy, but it allows for the attribution of comic rather than Christian faith to Carroll. Polhemous calls Carroll's comedy regressive, but he means by that a profound and not frivolous or escapist return to childish experience. He stresses Alice's curiosity and interest more than her anxiety, her fun in playing chess more than her urge to dominate. Polhemous notices that Alice laughs through her tears when threatened with going out like a candle. He makes much of the Gnat's question, "What sort of insects do you rejoice in?" since this "assumes that man's fate naturally includes rejoicing." For him, Carroll's animism excludes death, and his "death jokes are actually resurrection jokes" for they "transubstantiate dead bodies into living waves of joy—laughter." Polhemous allows a darker note to enter into his discussion of language and perhaps achieves his most convincing balance in showing Carroll's sense of both frustration and delight in words' multiplicity of meaning. Polhemous approves what Elizabeth Sewell disapproves in her landmark *The Field of Nonsense* (London: Chatto & Windus, 1952)—Carroll's inclination to turn all things to play and laughter as if he were his own God.

Heiterkeit quite glows in Polhemous, while a few other critics cast off glints of it. In *A Celebration* Nina Demurova's "Toward a Definition of *Alice's* Genre: The Folktale and Fairy-Tale Connections" aligns Carroll's work with a carnival laughter tradition. Unfortunately, this essay deteriorates into mistakes based on insufficient knowledge of Carroll's life and criticism in English about him. For instance, Demurova supposes that Dodgson lived by so complete a work ethic that he could not have meant to satirize the content of Watts's "Little Busy Bee." Jeffrey Stern's "Lewis Carroll the Surrealist" in *A Celebration* reminds us of the legacy of insouciance bequeathed by Carroll to the surrealists. Judith Little's "Liberated Alice; Dodgson's Female Hero as Domestic Rebel" in *Women's Studies,* 3, (1976), 195-205, lacks sophistication as an example of feminist literary criticism and lacks a sprightly touch, it must be said, growing a bit grim in associating the Queen of Hearts' fits with labor pains and questioning whether the White Knight remains as a pleasant memory for Alice. Little stresses Alice's resistance to the social roles of queen and mother, her disillusionment with chivalric knighthood, and her refusal to be part of the Red King's dream. But if not exactly heiter, Alice asserts herself and finds liberation.

A last essay to include here abounds in a sophistication and holds much interest, though it sometimes loses me. This is Gilles Deleuze's "The Schizophrenic and Language: Surface and Depth in Lewis Carroll and Antonin Artaud" in *Textual Strategies, Perspectives in Post-Structuralist Criticism,* ed. Josué V. Harari (Ithaca: Cornell Univ. Press, 1979), pp. 277-295. Deleuze demonstrates the difference between the language of Artaud's schizophrenic nonsense and Carroll's art of nonsense. According to an intricate argument concerning linguistic depth and surface, Carroll emerges as superficial, but "the organization of language is not separable from the poetic discovery of the surface.'' Deleuze advances some dubious ideas about the importance of a little girl's breaking of the surface, leaving the depths of the maternal body and as yet unaware of her own. Heiter in all this is the conclusion that Carroll does not collapse and engulf meaning in the nihilist manner of the schizophrenic. Deleuze counters the doubts of previous psychoanalytic critics as to Carroll's mental health.

While much recent interpretation may be ranged along the line between Angst, malice and Heiterkeit, there are other lines, and I can at least briefly indicate one by designating three literary-historical Carrolls—Victorian Carroll, Modernist Carroll, and Post-Modernist Carroll. Robert B. Henkle and Stephen Prickett give us versions of a Victorian Carroll in their *Comedy and Culture* and *Victorian Fantasy* (Bloomington and London: Indiana Univ. Press; Sussex: Harvester Press, 1979), respectively. Henkle places Carroll in the context of the humor and Prickett in that of the fantasy of the time. The latter work holds particular value in setting the historical record straight, since the importance of a nineteenth-century British fantasy tradition has till now received little recognition. Strangely, Henkle himself shows a want of such historical awareness in his essay in *A Celebration*, "Carroll's Narrative Underground: 'Modernism' and Form." Here he falls into the "insidious evolutionist fallacy of looking upon nineteenth-century works as precursors or developmental stages on the way to the modern novel," which he himself defines and aims to avoid. That is, he leaps forward to find counterparts to Carroll's form in modern work, rejecting significant generic alliance with Victorian children's literature and fantasy. Henkle might look closer to home, to Carroll's friend and fellow-fantasist George MacDonald, for instance, before taking such leaps forward, and backwards, to Bergson and Menippean satire. Prickett's book would prove a useful antidote here.

In his essay, Henkle belongs among those who cherish a Modernist Carroll. It seems fairest to do so without making him out a (welcome) exception to Victorian norms. Henkle's book sometimes seems out of sympathy with the age, and his essay certainly contains some unsympathetic remarks. In that Carroll did not demonstrably fall under the influence of Menippean satire, his "literary sensibility was often rather lamentable. He was not a literary man." Some further treatments of a Modernist Carroll include the Rackin essay and with it in *A Celebration*, Ann McGarrity Buki's "Lewis Carroll in *Finnegan's Wake*" and Jeffrey Stern's essay on Carroll and surrealism. Neither Buki nor Stern surprises us by aligning Carroll with Joyce and the surrealists, but Stern proves far more informative than Buki, whose argument remains at a superficial level (and not in Deleuze's sense of the word).

For a Post-Modernist Carroll we may note Deleuze again and consider in the *Celebration* volume Jean Gattégno's *"Sylvie and Bruno, or the Inside and the Outside,"* and Jan B. Gordon's "Lewis Carroll, the *Sylvie and Bruno* Books and the Nineties: The Tyranny of Textuality." There are also Irving Massey's chapter in *The Gaping Pig, Literature and Metamorphosis* (Berkeley, Los Angeles, London: Univ. of California Press, 1976) and Alwin L. Baum's "Carroll's *Alices,* the Semiotics of Paradox," *American Imago,* 34 (1977), 86-108. Binding these into a loose group are some tendency to place the *Sylvie and Bruno* books among Carroll's best, a preoccupation with issues of language, and a recognizable psychoanalytic/linguistic critical vocabulary. We find, here and there, Freud, de Saussure, Lacan, Derrida, universes of discourse, overdetermination of predication, signifier and signified, texts and textuality. However, I cannot forgive Baum for misspelling Liddell. Gattégno and Gordon locate great interest in formal devices for setting up dualities and then merging them in the *Sylvie and Bruno* books. Both of these critics suggest Carroll's fascination with a language of childhood linked with dreams and with freedom. Gordon contrasts the late novels with the *Alices* as explorations of an aged rather than youthful attitude toward language. Whereas the seven- to seven-and-a-half-year-old Alice wishes to grow up into a conventional linguistic order, the *Sylvie and Bruno* narrator is both old and sick and seeks escape from the entropy of linguistic self-consciousness by regress to a prelinguistic universe. Gordon finds the horrors of textuality in those passages which wonder whether people might eventually run out of originality, find that all had been said and nothing remained but reiteration. This essay symptomizes the malaise treated by Carroll. We are impressed and stultified by a compulsive referentiality. Hardly a detail in Carroll but finds its mirror elsewhere in literature or life. Everything here seems to lead to everything everywhere, from a goodly number of the classics of Western literature to the history of kindergarten and the teutonization of late nineteenth-century British culture. Gordon's essay analyzes and exemplifies the liability of language to set the very energy of signification into an entropic spin. Such may be the particularly acute liability of critical language, as the Post-Modernists show us. I may therefore seek comfort by turning from literary criticism as I conclude.

I can turn, at least, to studies of the pictures in Carroll's books. Of essays in *A Celebration* by Michael Hancher, Richard Kelly, Janis Lull, and Robert Dupree, the last is the best. I must confess I find it so because of its subtle interpretation of the interrelation between illustrations and text. Textuality is hard to resist. Dupree's "The White

Knight's Whiskers and the Wasp's Wig in *Through the Looking Glass"* discerns a sort of hair fetish in Carroll and from this gleans new insight on the White Knight and the conclusion that Tenniel should not have persuaded Carroll to eliminate the Wasp in the Wig. This essay contrasts with Lull's in suggesting some lack of harmony between author and illustrator. As Dupree develops his thesis, quite benign images of old age emerge and a benign understanding of Alice's relation to it, neither the age or sickness of the *Sylvie and Bruno* narrator nor Angst or malice on Alice's part.

Moving further away from criticism, I will mention some key artistic and philosophical reimaginings or appropriations. Barry Moser has produced highly acclaimed wood engravings for *Alice in Wonderland* (limited ed., Pennyroyal Press, to appear in a Univ. of California Press trade ed., 1982). French feminist thinkers and fiction writers have taken up Alice for their own purposes, as seen in Luce Irigaray's *Ce sexe qui n'en est pas un* (Paris: Minuet, 1977), and in Denise Le Dantec's *Les Joueurs de Go* (Stock, 1977). Linda Gillman provides a good introduction to this French material in "The Looking-Glass Through Alice" in *Gender and Literary Voice,* ed. Janet Todd (New York, London: Holmes & Meier, 1980). Alice enters into the musical sphere in David Del Tredici's very beautiful and important *Final Alice,* premiered by the Chicago Symphony in 1976 and available in a London recording (LDR71018, 1981). These works may all be grouped with Post-Modernism in point of period, at least. A number of Moser's pictures suggest the reverse of Heiterkeit, but Alice as a feminist symbol exposes not only dilemmas but positive potentialities, and Del Tredici pits anxious and violent-sounding dissonance and dislocation of rhythm against a lovely melodic line that seems to gain ground; *Final Alice* ends with an almost mystic sense of resolution.

NOTES ON CONTRIBUTORS

Nina Auerbach is the author of *Communities of Women* (1978) and *Woman and the Demon: The Life of a Victorian Myth* (Harvard, 1982). Among other articles, she has written "Alice and Wonderland: A Curious Child," which appeared in *Victorian Studies* (1973). When not in Wonderland, she is an Associate Professor of English at the University of Pennsylvania.

Kathleen Blake, Associate Professor of English, University of Washington. Author of *Play, Games, and Sport, The Literary Works of Lewis Carroll* and essays on Jean-Paul Richter, De Quincey, George Eliot, Hardy, Schreiner, Stevenson, and Barrie. Book forthcoming on *Love and the Woman Question in Victorian Literature, The Art of Self-Postponement.*

Beverly Clark teaches English at Wheaton College (Mass.), and has completed a study of *Reflections of Fantasy: The Mirror-Worlds of Carroll, Nabokov, and Pynchon.*

Morton N. Cohen, Professor Emeritus of the City University of New York, has spent the last twenty years working on Lewis Carroll. His edition of *The Letters of Lewis Carroll* (2 vols.) appeared in 1979. He is now at work on a biography of Carroll.

Robert Dupree is the author of, among other things, "The White Knight's Whiskers and the Wasp's Wig in *Through the Looking-Glass,*" and is completing a study of Lewis Carroll and modern education. He currently teaches at the University of Dallas.

Selwyn H. Goodacre, a British physician, has published numerous textual studies of Lewis Carroll's works. A Carroll collector of great distinction, he is the past Chairman of the Lewis Carroll Society (England) and is the long-time editor of *Jabberwocky: The Journal of the Lewis Carroll Society.*

Jan B. Gordon is Professor of English at Doshisha University in Kyoto, Japan. His previous work on Lewis Carroll includes two essays, "The *Alice* Books and the Metaphors of Victorian Childhood" and "Lewis Carroll, the *Sylvie and Bruno* Books, and the Nineties: The Tyranny of Textuality."

Edward Guiliano, co-editor of this collection, is also the editor of *Lewis Carroll Observed* (1976); *Lewis Carroll: A Celebration* (1982); *The Complete Illustrated Works of Lewis Carroll* (1982); and is the compiler of *Lewis Carroll: An Annotated International Bibliography* (1980). He teaches English at the New York Institute of Technology and writes regularly on Victorian and modern literature and art, and on other topics. He also edits *Dickens Studies Annual: Essays on Victorian Fiction.*

Peter Heath, an Oxford-trained philosopher, has taught at the University of Virginia since 1962. He lectures and writes regularly on Carroll and is the author of *The Philosopher's Alice* (1974). A bibliophile and Carroll collector, he is also the past President of the Lewis Carroll Society of North America.

James R. Kincaid has written the Introduction and Notes for The Pennyroyal Press editions of *Alice's Adventures in Wonderland* (1981) and *Through the Looking-Glass* (1982) (trade editions by the University of California Press, 1982 and 1983). He is the author of *Dickens and the Rhetoric of Laughter* (1971), *Tennyson's Major Poems* (1975), and *The Novels of Anthony Trollope* (1977), along with essays on Victorian literature and critical theory. He is Professor of English at the University of Colorado.

140

Joyce Carol Oates, who teaches at Princeton University, is the author most recently of *A Bloodsmoor Romance* (Dutton), and *Invisible Woman: New & Selected Poems 1970-82* (Ontario Review Press). She is a member of the American Academy and Institute of Arts and Letters.

Donald Rackin, Professor of English at Temple University, is the author of numerous articles on Lewis Carroll, including "Alice's Journey to the End of Night," and editor of *Alice's Adventures in Wonderland: A Critical Handbook* (1969). He is also the editor of *Academe,* the journal of the American Association of University Professors.